My Kinsale

An Anthology

Edited by Alannah Hopkin

ORLA KELLY PUBLISHING

ISBN 978-1-912328-23-9
© *2018 by Words by Water. All rights reserved.*

This book is copyright under the Berne Convention. All intellectual property rights including copyright, design right and publishing rights rest with the contributors. No part of this book may be copied, reproduced, stored or transmitted in any way including any written, electronic, recording, or photocopying without written permission of the contributors. Although precaution have been taken to verify the accuracy of the information contained herein, the contributors, editor and publisher assume no responsibility for any errors or omissions. No liability is assumed for damages that may result from the use of information contained within. Published in Ireland by Orla Kelly Publishing. Edited by Alannah Hopkin. Printed by ePrint. Photo credits: Front Cover: Cathal O'Connor - The Pier. Back Cover: Alannah Hopkin - Scilly. All illustrations contained within are reproduced by kind permission of the contributors listed.

Orla Kelly Publishing
27 Kilbrody, Mount Oval,
Rochestown, Cork,

Map of Kinsale (courtesy of The Collins Press)

CONTENTS

(Contributors in order of appearance)

Chasing the Dream

Rod Hunt	7
Siobhan Waldron	7
Veronica Holley	8
Linda Ibbotson	11
Peter W. Frey	13
Alan Clayton	17
John Young	19
Afric McGlinchey	22
Paul Moody	24
Derek Mahon	25

Kinsale at Work

Martin Shanahan	33
Jerome Lordan	35
Brian Cronin	37
Adrian Wistreich	41
Charlotte Cargin	43
Barry Moloney	46

Contributors Cont.

Kinsale Community

Malcolm Hall	51
Elizabeth Creed	53
Paul Eaton	59
Christina Broderick	60
Dearbhail Connon	62
Alannah Hopkin	63
Sheila Forde	66

Photographs

Historical Kinsale

John Thuillier	173
Fergal Browne	175
Brian Lalor	180
Klaus Harvey	183
Bernard McGouran	186
Dermot Ryan	192
Fergal Browne	193

Contributors Cont.

Kinsale Memories

Cristina Galvin	201
Sheila Forde	204
Robin Renwick	208
George Harding	210
Augustus Young	214
Donal Herlihy	217
William Hall	218
Netta Murray	223
Ann Daly	225
Matthew Geden	228
Lynn Harding	229

Outdoor Kinsale

Adrian Wistreich	233
Cara McDonagh	236
Daniel Galvin	238
Marcia Wrixon	241
Grace O'Doherty	242

Contributors Cont.

Outdoor Kinsale

Sheila Forde	244
Kevin Cahill	246
Alannah Hopkin	251
Gemma Tipton	253
George Harding	257

Thanks from the Words by Water festival to the following for allowing us to use their images.

Alannah Hopkin; Adrian Wistreich; Giles Norman; Brian Lalor; Caoimhe Nace; Cathal O'Connor; Dermot Ryan; Michael Prior; Debbie Morris; Peter Frey; Dave Fannin; Teresa O Donnell; Margaret Waller; Joachim Beug; Tomas Liniecki; Ben O Donnell; Paul Deane; Conor McCloskey; Katherine Boucher Beug; Alice Tallent; Harry Dunnican; Neil Payne; Pamela Hardesty; Claire Keating; Katherine Beug; Norma Mulligan; Georgina Sutton; Aileen Hurley; Sheena Jolley.

living in Soho in the centre of London, so I went from one extreme to another.

I remember soon after the move, standing at the bottom of the Stoney Steps on my way to Barrett's the butcher's, and wondering where they led to, and whether I would ever nip up and down them with the same ease as the locals. I had a shock on my first walk around Compass Hill – coming back into town through Ballinacubby, I thought I had lost my way and arrived at another village that was not Kinsale at all. The narrow smugglers' lane just beyond Commogue that goes uphill from the river to Cappagh was another exciting exploration, as I learnt the geography of my new home by exploring it on foot.

The real breakthrough came when I moved from Summercove to the Dutch House in Cork Street, and became a true Kinsalite. Around about the same time, as a locally-based journalist, I took on the court reporting for the *Irish Examiner*, and also covered meetings of Kinsale Urban District Council – both providing many hours of entertainment and education.

I discovered that there was a part of Kinsale called 'the flat of town', and that its residents had a different accent from the residents of Scilly, who differed again from the Worlds Enders who, I was told, 'ad a strange way with haitches'. I got to know the lads who passed the time of day outside the Temperance Hall by name, and they in turn gave me the great honour of a town nickname – Cher – presumably because I had long dark hair. I moved house only once in Kinsale, and swore never again, so I have lived in the same house now for thirty years.

Whether any of this qualifies me to edit an anthology entited My Kinsale I do not know. Probably not, but I've given it my best shot. It has been a pleasure sorting through the photographs and reading about other people's Kinsales, present, past and to come. It is good to

Introduction

Alannah Hopkin

For a long time My Kinsale was just Summercove, where my mother Angela Foley grew up and went to Summercove School, and the peninsula beyond – Bawnavota, Sally Port, Middle Cove, Lower Cove, Preghane and Ballymacus.

My mother emigrated twice, first in 1932, when she and her sister Sheila went to London to train as nurses. In those economically depressed times there was nothing for them here. That is where she met and married my father, Denis Hopkin, an English doctor. After the end of the War (or The Emergency) she and my father came back to Cork, but there was no suitable work for my father, and in 1953 they emigrated to London. After her death, my grandmother's house in Summercove became the family holiday home. Summercove meant holidays, usually summer ones, and a different set of friends and relations from my London ones. The furthest east I ventured was the ruins of the haunted hotel on the Lower Road, one of my favourite playgrounds. Kinsale was where the grown-ups went to do the shopping and go to Mass. As the youngest in the family, I was excused both outings, so I hardly knew Kinsale until I moved to Summercove year-round in 1982, in order to write. At the time I was

Submitting entries to the next edition.

If you would like to contribute material to the next edition, email us at formykinsale@gmail.com. Write a short story, historic piece or memoir in less than 1000 words, using Word, and email it as an attachment to formykinsale@gmail.com. Send us a poem about Kinsale (maximum 25 lines). Send us photographs by email – black and white or colour – ideally 1-5MB file size in Jpeg format to formykinsale@gmail.com. Name each image with your name then the title of the picture. In your email, include your name, how long you've lived in or near Kinsale – were you born in Kinsale, how far back does your family association with the town go, or what is your association with Kinsale?

Buying copies in print or for download.

Printed copies of My Kinsale will continue to be available locally in the book shops, and it is also possible to order them through any one of 68 online retailers, including Amazon, Kobo and many others. If you would like to purchase a copy for download to your e-reader, all these retailers offer this service.

If you have an enquiry about this book, please email Adrian Wistreich at formykinsale@gmail.com.

Adrian Wistreich

Words By Water

Clár Éire Ildánach
*Creative Ireland
Programme
2017–2022*

Cork County Council
Comhairle Contae Chorcaí

Foreword

My Kinsale

This is a Kinsale community project which sets out to record the stories, memories and opinions of residents and those with a special connection to our town. This project is an initiative of Words By Water, Kinsale's literary festival, now in its second year. We've decided to produce a print and electronic book this year, and to set up an ongoing archive of contributions online. It is important not to lose details of our local history, or the stories of those who move away. It is important to the cohesion of our community that we share our experiences of the town, and My Kinsale aims to capture as much material as possible.

We are publishing My Kinsale in association with the Kinsale Chamber of Tourism and Business, in order to help reach the diaspora, those who regularly visit our town, and those who are planning to visit and would like to understand our ways a little before they arrive.

This first edition lays down the first layer of content for a cultural archive including photographic and written histories of Kinsale, its people and place, including creative and factual written work. It contains creative input from people of all ages, including short commentaries, stories, poems and historical information about Kinsale.

We have received funding from Creative Ireland, and the project is being supported by Words By Water, as part of our annual festival. Sales of the book will not only help to underwrite this first edition, but hopefully will contribute to funding for updates in future years.

Our thanks go to Alannah Hopkin and Orla Kelly for their professional editing and production of the book, and to the forty or so contributors for their writing and images.

see that the community spirit which is such a strong feature of the town continues to change and develop, as new people move in, and the older generation pass on. The people who live in Kinsale, whether natives or blow-ins, are united by the belief that it is the best possible place in the world to live, and I hope that this anthology conveys that message clearly.

Thank you to the committee of the Words by Water Festival for inviting me to put this anthology together; to Kinsale Chamber of Tourism and Cork County Council and the Creative Ireland Programme 2017-2022 for helping to fund it; and to all the people of Kinsale and its diaspora who contributed to its content.

Alannah Hopkin

Kinsale, 2018

Chasing the Dream

Contributor: Rod Hunt

Hi, I'm Rod Hunt and I've been in this love affair with Kinsale since my wife, Norma, and I first set foot on the Pier in 1973. Kinsale was recommended to us by the then bartender at the Eccles Hotel in Glengarriff, and I'm indebted to her for life.

Mrs Richardson was our landlady at The Skillet, Mary at the Tap Tavern saw to our liquid needs, as did the folks at the Grey Hound. Later, following Norma's passing in 2003, I was hosted by the gracious and hospitable Tony and Colette Boland in their townhouse and following that I've been furnished with quarters in the Shearwater by Jim Good, virtually over the Vista, and am keen on Colette's seafood chowder.

The late Eugene Gillen and I wrote a book together called, *Sinking the Lusitania,* and I've written three other books while living there. I'm a gold miner in the Yukon Territory of Canada and raise Sport Horses in Minnesota, and I am active in that business in Ireland.

I've travelled to, visited, enjoyed time in 66 countries of this world and Kinsale will always be my favourite over all.

Contributor: Siobhan Waldron and her husband Gavin Ryan run the Black Pig Wine Bar in Lower O'Connell Street, Kinsale.

The Black Pig

My husband and I moved to Kinsale six years ago, one dark and cold January night, our whole lives packed into our ancient Mercedes. The dream of opening our own little wine bar was about to become a reality. We had always loved visiting Kinsale, now this time we were staying for good (if they'd have us…).

During the busy summer months when this lovely town is full of life and visitors from far off places, I think how lucky I am to call this special place my home. But also, too, in the quiet and dark winter months, when life slows down, I love living here.

Now our son is three years old, growing up beside the sea, in a warm and caring community. He is from Kinsale, which makes us feel that we belong here that little bit more.

We will never leave. This is our home.

Contributor: Veronica Holley was born in South Wales, where she gained first class Honours in Creative Writing. She has contributed articles and short stories to various magazines and journals over the years, and written a book, plays and pantomimes for schools. She spent seven years in Africa before moving to Kent in South East England. She has recently moved to Kinsale with her husband, and is a member of the a capella choir, Kinsale Voices. She also plays alto saxophone with the Bandon Concert Band. She is currently working on a science fiction novel for older children.

Rise and plunge, rise and plunge, the ferry boat slapped its way through heavy, post-hurricane seas, heading for the sheltering harbour of Rosslare. On board, I curled up on my bunk, racked with seasickness. I reckoned my cat Amelie was probably dead by now, her lifeless form lying prostrate on the back seat of our car down on the lower deck where we'd been advised to keep her safe. Beyond the heaving seas Ireland lay beneath impenetrable darkness.

It was not the glorious arrival I had envisioned.

After hours of wretchedness, our car finally rolled off the ferry onto Irish soil. Amelie proved to be still alive, so we headed west towards Kinsale. Everywhere lay evidence of the hurricane's brutal passage; trees knocked to the ground, lights punched out, candlelight quivering through darkened windows, shops shuttered and barred. Would our house still be standing? Would its roof be missing? Would it be in darkness? We were travelling strangers, ghosts drifting through a stricken land, fugitives from our own.

What had brought us here from Wales to Ireland – and to Kinsale in particular? Brexit was the catalyst. I'll never forget how our Prime Minister Theresa May referred to people like us – British people who wanted to remain members of the EU – as, "citizens of nowhere". This insult struck the final blow, coming swiftly after the initial shock of the Brexit vote in 2016. The devastating impact of all this is almost impossible to describe. We began to feel like strangers in our own country. More disturbing was the ominous increase in flag flying and racist attacks against law-abiding citizens. Half the country seemed set against the other half. We no longer felt free to express our views in public.

When my great-grandfather, Thomas Walsh left Cork behind him and crossed the Irish Sea with his wife and son at the height of the potato famine (1845-49), he didn't know what awaited him in Wales. Buoyed up by the hope that his situation must improve for it could surely get no worse, he was determined to make a new life for himself and his small family. Two generations later, my mother Josephine Walsh, together with her sister and two brothers were raised in the same place Thomas had made his home. It was by this time, a lively Irish community in Swansea, South Wales. The children were taught by Irish nuns at the local convent and believed themselves to be as Irish as their grandfather.

During the last war the whole area was heavily bombed, destroying the tight rows of terraced houses, the Dublin Arms, (the pub my mother's parents used to run), and even the local Catholic

Church. I'm grateful for the fact that although it obliterated every last trace of the community, my mother kept it alive by regaling me with colourful incidents from her own childhood there, and recounting tales about her grandfather Thomas Walsh.

I remember how vividly she would describe the St. Patrick's Day procession led by Thomas, mounted on a magnificent white charger. The whole community would gather together at the Dublin Arms, the children dressed in traditional Irish costumes of white and green, and the band would strike up a lively tune. This signalled the march down the hill from the Irish houses into the centre of town and along the bustling high street, crowds of shoppers cheering and smiling as they passed by. You can imagine how much I loved these stories and naturally drew close to Ireland during the telling of them. Subsequently, I spent several magical holidays in Ireland both with my parents, and with Michael and our children, so it was no leap of logic to turn to Ireland as the country I most wanted to make my new home. Fortunately, he too had fallen under the spell of Ireland – particularly since the discovery of Kinsale.

Searching for a house in Ireland, when living in another country was not easy. Initially we explored the area around Cork, thinking Cobh might be a good place to live, so we chose to spend our Christmas there while we viewed potential properties. Not fully convinced, we settled on Kinsale for our next visit to Ireland, simply because it seemed to be a strategic centre from which to explore the coast in search of more houses to view. We had never visited Kinsale before, so we expected a sleepy fishing village with nothing much going on. How wrong we were!

'What prevents us from settling here?', we asked each other, delighted to have found such a beautiful place, so lively, multicultural, friendly and outgoing. Fired with enthusiasm, we sold our house,

Michael finalised the sale of his business in London's financial district (all not without incident), and we bought a house just outside the village.

What exactly is the real Kinsale? The real Kinsale is, for us, a safe haven in which to recuperate from the upheaval in our lives, happy in the knowledge that, at last, we're living in a sane, open and tolerant society.

In a final twist, after living here for several weeks, I was amazed to learn that Kinsale is twinned with Mumbles, the village where I was born and raised. Surely fate had secretly taken a hand! Thomas Walsh would have been so pleased with this completing of the circle, from his own fateful journey across the Irish Sea to Wales, to the return at last, of one of his descendants to her ancestral homeland.

Contributor: Linda Ibbotson is a poet, artist and photographer from the UK, currently residing in Co. Cork, Ireland. Her poetry, artwork and photography has been published internationally including Levure Litteraire, Enchanting Verses, Literary Review, Irish Examiner, California Quarterly, Fekt, Live Encounters, Sermos Galica, PB7 and forthcoming Poethead, has also been read on radio, and performed in France by Irish musician and actor Davog Rynne.

She writes a poetry and arts blog Contemplating the Muse.

Homage to Kinsale

As nights obsidian curtain lifted,
the skylark heralds the dawn chorus
in my demesne of duck egg blue.
From my balcony,
a mirage of matchstick masts
navigate the thirsty mouth of the harbour,
and my skin drinks it all in.
Sometimes, when I bury myself, in myself.
never quite reaching the point when thinking stops,
I unlatch the door, drink tea, and savour wild berry tart
at Poets Corner,
or stroll to the Spaniard
where the swans dance to Francesca's mandolin
and in my solitude, I feel quietly content.
I look at life in black and white at The Gallery,
buy a chiffon scarf from Stone Mad,
peacock feathers with hand stitched beads
and fly it like a kite on the beach.
After sundown you'll find me in The Black Pig
sipping a glass of red,
satisfied with the feeling that finally,
I have arrived.

Contributor: Peter Frey is an American motoring journalist who, after forty years in the warm sunshine of California and Florida, moved to Kinsale to develop his appreciation of a different climate... and a different kind of writing.

Credit: Bord Fáilte

Some Automotive Aspects of Our Irish Adventure

We, my bride of 29 years and I, made the unlikely move from Florida to Kinsale almost two years ago. After shivering through six months of Irish winter in a draughty but scenic rented house across from the Bulman, the lease came due and rather than returning to our warm home across the Atlantic, we surprised ourselves – and everyone who knew us by buying a house here. Giddy with the promise of calling Kinsale home and spending our golden years exploring Ireland and Europe, we sold our Florida condo (the one with the elevator to the beach, two heated swimming pools and the balcony that provided a front-row seat for God's own sunset every night), and recently became full-time residents.

Now, after a forty-year career as an automotive journalist spent driving the world's best cars on the world's most interesting and challenging roads, I've been smacked in the face by the necessity of buying a big red 'L' for my windshield and working my way through the arcane process of getting my Irish driver's license.

Just now beginning to deal with the various realities of living our Irish dream, I was reminded of a story I had written for an American newspaper after our first vacation in Ireland a few years ago, back when it was all romance, rented cars and driving from one fancy hotel to another. Ah, those were the days...

It started this infatuation of mine with the endlessly entertaining emerald roller coaster ride that is driving in Ireland during a car-crazy youth spent on the serpentine asphalt legend high above Los Angeles called Mulholland Drive. It acquired a new dimension with the idyllic cinematic imagery of 'The Quiet Man,' and became a vivid reality during my first experience with the Ring of Kerry.

Clouds, yes, and often rain. The occasional moment of terror as, on a road barely wide enough for one car, you encounter a hurtling tourist bus or a lumbering farm tractor. But somehow you survive. And, just over the next rise, a castle on the edge of a lake, a valley full of flowers, the sweeping vista of mountains rising from a tapestry of farms stitched together with ancient stone walls.

Hugging the side of a mountain, suspended halfway between sea and sky, find yourself in awe of the cathedral tunnels of ancient trees curving overhead, venerating the vision of gothic churches around every turn, enchanted by tiny villages so perfect that they might be post cards propped up by the side of the road. And all the while basking in a sense of history so pervasive and palpable it feels like you're slaloming around a thousand years of ghosts and legends.

And, for those who appreciate such things, every few seconds the fierce, precise joy of driving a good car fast on mostly empty roads that curve and climb and dive like some particularly agile and energetic bird practicing for the flock's sunset acrobatics.

There are a lot of beautiful places to drive in the world, but few that offer such pleasures in such a concentrated form. And when the time comes to stop for the night, the people are friendly, the beer is good, the whiskey better and the food heavenly.

Such is the romance of driving in Ireland. Now for a few practical tips.

There are highways between the cities, but stick to those and you miss the best part. <u>Back Roads Ireland</u> from Eyewitness Travel is both bible and time machine, the gospel of a simpler, better world that appears when you take that side road instead of going straight.

If you only have time to 'do' Ireland instead of a leisurely exploration, do the 'Ring of Kerry', 111 miles of the best of what Ireland has to offer in a one-day drive. Fly into Dublin, take the train to Cork, rent a car, find a hotel in Kinsale (the first stop on an even more epic, 1600-mile drive called The Wild Atlantic Way)… and set forth. The tour busses travel counter-clockwise, and since you'll want to take in the scenery anyway, better to follow one than have to dodge dozens heading toward you.

Ireland is a small country with a Byzantine road system, so rent a small car; an Audi A4 is the perfect combination of size and luxury. And get the insurance, and a navigation system. Google Maps on your iPhone will get you there, but it lacks imagination; in-car nav systems seem to delight in getting you there via the scenic route.

It's not all countryside and the cities and towns are more crowded than almost anything you'll find here, Manhattan at rush hour included. If you want some practice, head for the nearest shopping mall parking lot a few days before Christmas.

And finally, no, that's neither me nor my Irish bride in the red convertible, though we have driven a car like that like that on roads like that. It's a photo from the Ireland Tourism web site. But, in this instance at least, the reality is more than a match for the marketing.

A Thousand Thundering Farewells

Separated from my tranquil green home

by a thousand thundering farewells,

every one, in retrospect,

taking on the aspect of a blade,

slicing my leafy glade into emerald pieces.

What strange forces hold court,

offering leases but not ownership,

respite, but not rest,

something worth having,

but not the best,

a relief from the roam, but still

a thousand thundering farewells from home.

How then to achieve, to vanquish

this need to leave? Stay?

Live life day by day in the same place,

knowing every face and secret

in most intimate detail?

Eschew the road, the rail, the trail,

the hail from strangers well-met?

Simple, and yet, at a cost, horizons lost,

fluid become frost, momentum yielding

to that certain shade of green,

>   a vista seen to encompass
>   a thousand years of history,
>   tumbled stones a mystery
>   and the song of birds at dawn
>   overpowering the roar of both
>   farewells and that far-distant shore.

Contributor: Alan Clayton moved to Kinsale in 1996. He writes: My wife Gwenn, née Brannigan has a mother who comes from Cork, and had spent many summers in the area with her cousins. We ended up in Kinsale because in 1995 we had no home and no kids, and we went on holiday to Parknasilla. It was so sunny, it was like the Med. So back in the UK we subscribed to the <u>Examiner</u> property pages (it was pre-Internet), and came back six months later, renting an apartment in Kinsale to start the house hunting from and buy our dream home.

They Say Everything Happens for a Reason

In the 22 years that have followed, it feels like the community that prides itself on good food and keeping itself tidy not only welcomed us, but insisted we enjoy the total immersion experience that is all too rare in other communities, and I've lived in a few!

Where else could you sit on a town council as a foreign passport holder, and unable to speak the native language. (I was the Green Party representative on Kinsale Town Council).

Where else would circumstances conspire for your wife to give birth in the en-suite bathroom so your daughter can claim to be a 110% Kinsale native?

Kinsale is the kind of place where there's enough familiar faces to make me feel I belong, and enough strange faces to make me feel it's not finished yet.

Kinsale is a work in progress. I know that because half the restaurants have been here for ever, and half re-open each summer under new management. Indeed, half the people have been here for ever, and half have landed recently. Like me in 1996, they now find themselves under new management – and they mostly don't know how lucky they are.

I also know Kinsale isn't finished because:

- the traffic restrictions don't apply on Sunday – the only day you need them!

- there are a growing number of churches but less people attending!

- rent for loyal local labour shot up 50% in the last 3 years while their wages went up 10%!

- the last butcher (preceded by the baker and the candlestick maker) is disappearing (in the gourmet capital!!) because we all want him, but not to BE him!

So, yes, I am frustrated Kinsale isn't finished yet. But if frustration is a sign that I care, then that's a good thing.

And my cause for hope lies in something that didn't exist back in 1996. The 'sharing economy'. The community I feel part of today is beyond magical when it comes to sharing. It is caring for neighbours in an almost spiritual way, although not everyone would express it in those terms. I can only imagine what that would look like if we did the same in a mightily material way.

So, if you want to borrow my car tomorrow – it's yours for $20. I'm going off to train as a butcher.

Contributor: John Young was born in Glasgow and travelled widely in the course of his career as a Medical Equipment engineer, living for extended periods in the Middle East, Khazakhstan and Russia. He was a keen scuba diver in his youth. He holds the Yachtmaster Ocean qualification, and worked as a skipper for Sail Ireland. He still keeps his yacht on Kinsale Yacht Club Marina. He has published two novels, The Scottish Armada and The Crescent (writing as Chris Merle) – see Amazon.co.uk. He has lived in Kinsale since 1997.

John Young

Kinsale? Never heard of it!

Somewhat reluctantly, I handed over ten American dollars for my pint of Guinness. 'Pajzollsta!'. The year was 1996, the pub was the Shamrock, and the city was Moscow. It was only five years after Perestroika, the collapse of Communism, and already the skyline was filling up with adverts for Heineken with many others to follow.

The Guinness was not bad, the chemicals used to keep it fresh did take away the fond memories I had when I had visited the brewery in Dublin. The Irish had not wasted any time in cashing in on the collapse and the upsurge of consumerism. There was already an Irish supermarket on the Arbat, a major highway leading from the Kremlin, ten lanes wide to allow tanks and the military a quick escape. Now neon signs from the west proclaimed their freedom message to the populace.

The Shamrock was one of several Irish pubs springing up to slake the thirst of the Muscovite and many expats like myself who were drafted in to take advantage of this new Mecca. The manager was Irish and fluent in Russian, the bar staff were Russian, attractive, and trained to pour Guinness to perfection. Needless to say, the pub was popular with the many expats working there.

I was originally from Scotland, and as a Medical Equipment engineer I had spent several years in the Middle East with varying experiences from boredom to panic.

Now I was in Moscow and about as far away from the sea as I have ever been. The sea was one of my major loves in this life, and I was missing it badly. I had been lucky enough to join the Moscow Sailing Club, and to my knowledge was the only European to join it. My status was not even given to the racing authorities. I remained below decks as our yacht was registered for the day's racing in the vast lakes north of Moscow, linked to the canal system from St Petersburg. Frequently our race was interrupted by a hydrofoil powering through en route to the capital, causing a certain amount of consternation in the crew, occasionally verging on panic.

However, I digress.

One rather slow day in the Shamrock I chatted to the manager. 'You know I am actually half-Irish'. My mother's folks had left the North and settled in Glasgow.

I had always been fascinated by the South, especially the Southwest, which always struck me as being fiord-like. I discussed my interests, diving, sailing, fishing and game sports. He smiled and said the immortal words which changed my life forever.

'Why don't you come to Kinsale! It's fantastic.'

'Where?'

'Kinsale. It's a small town near Cork on the estuary of the River Bandon,' and he went on to give me a description of the town. It frankly sounded magic!

I wrote to the Irish Embassy, who were most helpful and sent me maps, leaflets etc. extolling the virtues of the town. I was hooked!

Two years later my contract was finished, but Kinsale was still on my mind.

I was staying with a friend in Bournemouth in May, and while reading the local newspaper I saw an advert for the Swansea-Cork ferry, a special deal! And to a Scot this was irresistible. So I bought a ticket and drove to Swansea. In the bar, on the ferry, I heard several passengers talking, and heard the magic word, 'Kinsale'. I asked if they were going there: 'Too right! We are the Vintage Car Club from Wales and we go to Kinsale every year'.

'Can I follow you?'

'Certainly, if you don't mind driving at twenty miles an hour!'

So, that is how I entered Kinsale at twenty miles an hour on a glorious May day in 1997. As we entered the town, I said out loud, 'He's right!!', the manager of the pub in Moscow.

And as we all know, the rest is history. I returned to Scotland, sold up all my possessions, only keeping enough to fill five suitcases. I set sail in my yacht, berthed at Castlepark Marina, and lived on her for ten years. I am still here in my version of paradise and will never leave.

Contributor: Afric McGlinchey: Born in Galway, raised in various countries in Africa, I returned to Ireland in 1999, with my Zimbabwean husband and two children. We knew we wanted to find a home by the sea but hadn't chosen a specific location. We had bought a little Citroen 2CV and drove along the coast from Westport, looking for a place that felt right for us all. At sunset on the third day, we reached Kinsale. The yachts tinkling on pink silk water, the higgledy-piggledy colourful houses and winding lanes won us over instantly. We spent ten of my most memorable years there, the longest I've lived anywhere. Life changes took me further west, but Kinsale is always going to be home for me.

The Shift

I'm near the edge of a shift to a different stage; feel ok

with that, comforted by quiet sounds, drips of rain into

the watering can outside, rolling Rs of the fridge, so guttural

and French, and sometimes I pause to rock my neck, hear

things move from ear to ear, like loose change in the brain.

On Tuesdays there's the ceremony of the market,

where awnings ripple like silk tents, offering exotics:

kalamata olives and *boerewors*, fine cheeses and crêpes.

Or I cycle in the warm wind to the dock, passing men and boys

on the bridge, casting lines, eyes distant with concentration.

Masts in the marina clack, and hulls rock softly.

I like this town's sprightliness in autumn as the wind combs

through her knotted streets, sea lapping at her feet.

I like it when the boys pile around my kitchen table,
the muscular weave of their arms slung along chair backs,

streel of boisterous banter and Chinese takeaways, later
abandoned for willow-flick movements along moon-creased ledges.
I rummage through leftovers, my fear washed downriver
with a glass of wine. You skype, ask me to drive west tomorrow,
and we'll go sailing, fish for mackerel, fetch tomatoes from your tunnel.

I love our slow time, rhythms of our talk, butterfly thoughts
fused into dragons that shoot flaming ideas into the night.
For now the night curls round me, like a cat, and I'm glad
that I threw away my TV, that my house isn't haunted,
or inhabited by mice, and that sometimes I hear

a cough or next door's grandfather clock.
I listen in bed to the sweep of night rain, dampening
the earth like soaked bread, hungry plants reaching
for a mouthful. I leave the window open,
invite the night in, pay attention.

Contributor: Paul Moody lived and worked in the north of England before moving in mid-life to Castlepark House near the Dock Bar. With thanks to Brendan.

Brendan the Bread changed my life

It was a dark and dirty March Wednesday night in 1969 when I arrived into Kinsale, a travelling salesman in my Ford Cortina, looking for somewhere to stay. I found my way to the door of Acton's Hotel and checked in for a very lonely night as the only guest.

The following day was bright and chill, which after a miserable ten days travelling the country from north to south was a relief. This was my first visit to Kinsale and Ireland and I was intrigued by both the country and the friendly people.

I went walking by the river, not knowing where I was going or why. At a cottage near the old bridge I stopped to talk to Timmy Martin, who was hanging out at his gate and curious as to who was out walking this particular fine morning. We exchanged greetings and chatted as a van drew up to the front. 'Brendan take this young fellah out to the Old Head', he said, and I was soon bumping along in the van smelling the bread and feeling happy.

Brendan had his deliveries to do and his own curiosities about me as we stopped and started around the Old Head. The sky was brilliant blue, and merged with the sea that sparkled that day and I was entranced. His last delivery was at the Dock where I thanked him with a glass, little realising that Brendan had changed my life forever, and that this bar would be my local one day. He drove me back to Acton's Hotel, as it would have been a long walk in the days before the bridge. I still have no idea what his surname was, but when I told my story to a meeting of the Kinsale Historical Society they all named him as 'Brendan the Bread'.

I went on to travel the world trading in equipment for the food and beverage industries. I've been in over 60 countries in the course of my work but would return to Kinsale at every opportunity to hide away for 'me time'. My midlife crisis duly arrived and the solution was clear: go live in Kinsale, and life changed in a positive way.

Our home since 1990 is in Castlepark near the Dock. I married my wife Wendy in Kinsale, and our children were all born in the Bons Secours Hospital in Cork – Annabel in 1993, Camilla in 1994, William in 1996 and Katrina in 1997. We threw ourselves into many clubs, societies and causes, we were welcomed into the community and made so many lifelong friends despite being 'blow-ins' from over the water.

Kinsale has changed over the years, as we all have, and we share great memories with so many about how it used to be, though there is no desire to wind back the clock. We now have so many newbies in town who are having a positive effect on supporting our causes, organisations and local businesses, and we all share a love for this special place on earth.

Contributor: The poet Derek Mahon first visited Kinsale with friends from Trinity College, Dublin, in 1961 He has lived here at various times since, and continuously since 2001. He has received numerous awards including the Irish Academy of Letters Award, the Scott Moncrieff Translation Prize and the David Cohen Prize for Literature. Recent titles from the Gallery Press include <u>New Collected Poems</u>, <u>Olympia and the Internet</u> and <u>Against the Clock</u>.

This is a piece he wrote about Kinsale in 1987 for the Dublin magazine <u>Image</u>, which was reprinted in <u>Red Sails</u> (Gallery Press, 2014). He says: 'Despite a facetious tone and some anachronisms, I think it still catches something of the spirit of the place, though it's changed a bit since then.'

'Are you married or do you live in Kinsale?' This handsome resort on the Irish Riviera, eighteen miles due south of Cork and ten from the a*erphort*, has long been considered a den of iniquity. No smoke without fire, of course, and Kinsale's attitude in these matters would differ noticeably from that of Timoleague for example; yet, like everywhere else, Kinsale voted no in the recent divorce referendum [anachronism]. Beneath its raffish surface it's really quite an ordinary market town, differing from Timoleague only in this, that raffishness is one of its principal industries. Others include history, tourism, sailing, high kitchen and the consumption of wines. The nearby airport, more like an old-fashioned aerodrome [anachronism], the magnificent natural harbour and the proliferation of yacht races sponsored by *Le Figaro* and Budweiser [anachronism], have ensured a constant coming and going of Brits, Continentals and Americans, besides more recent economic migrants, some of whom have settled here, whence its cosmopolitan reputation. A handful, the Europeans especially, have an air of being wanted for raffishness in their own countries, which adds a touch of mystery and romance. Yet when I told the London publisher Tim O'Keeffe, himself a son of the town, that I was thinking of moving here and remarked on how 'handy' it was (meaning I could be in London, door to door, in less than three hours), he observed drily, 'Yes, very handy for Belgooly' – his way of reminding me that I was talking about Ireland ... Handy too for all kinds of social life. Shortly after my arrival I received an invitation from the novelist Alannah Hopkin: 'Round Up the Usual Suspects! A Party, a Celebration, a Charade, in the Spirit and Style of *Casablanca*. Dress: in the mood.' Deciding I wouldn't make a very good Bogie, I settled instead for Peter Lorre (Ugarte in the film), found an Egyptian fly-whisk, and snuck over there. Alannah shared a house then with Cork musicians, and I arrived to find one playing 'As Time Goes By' on a reconditioned harpsichord. A video of the movie was shown in an upstairs room, and towards midnight the fast set appeared. Before leaving I was issued with an exit visa, made out in

French and German on behalf of the Vichy government and the Third Reich (the attention to detail!) by a man from Bantry sporting a *pince-nez*. It seemed like an initiation into Kinsale society. There was a yellow RR at the gate as I left in the moonlight.

But Kinsale society is an older and more complex thing, dating back to the De Courcys and Roches of Norman times who founded the borough, having first bashed the McCarthys who ruled these parts. There was another bad fight at Knockrobin, north of the town, in December 1601, when Pat and Mick hacked vainly at the well-organized Brit in icy fog while prudent Spaniards sat drinking rum-and-Coke in the bar of Acton's Hotel [anachronism], uncertain whether or not to intervene. They didn't, like sensible men, and the Tudor conquest of Ireland was complete. Some years later, in 1690, James II sailed from here into French exile, pursued to the waterline by Williamite forces under Marlborough. Kinsale is ambiguously proud of these shameful incidents, as if the provision of a *mise-en-scène* were in itself matter for congratulation. A garrison town until 1921, it retains a slight flavour of Devon-and-Cornwall; English voices are frequently heard, and go with the Georgian architecture. The town has retained its famous old-world charm, all local slate and winding streets. Boat life adds a vicarious sense of adventure: you might wake to find the Asgard [anachronism) or a huddle of trawlers tied up at the quay, a Norwegian freighter at anchor. Certainly the Sibyl will be there [anachronism], a Bermuda-rigged yawl dating back to the 19th century, besides more recent creations – *Blithe Spirit, Flamingo, Moonraker* — some of them not so much boats as floating video games. Once there was great sea-angling here, but not any more: too expensive, or maybe the shark have wised up. The *Lusitania* still lies on the sea floor off the Old Head of course, and a Lusitania Grill, its name chosen with fastidious good taste, does fish 'n' chips at the pier (anachronism); which brings me to grub, the other thing Kinsale is famous for. The trouble about being famous for something is that you get self-conscious about it, so you end up with deplorable manifestations like the, dare I say, rather showy Gourmet Festival which consumes the citizenry, and visitors from Cork and farther afield (Montreal, Cape Town) during the first week of October. The time has come for Kinsale to get over its preoccupation with grub. The Gourmet Festival should be turned into an Arts Festival, with food on the side where it belongs. There's enough art going on from Youghal to Allihies to fill a dozen galleries; let the champagne and the lobsters take their turn! [Anachronism: there's been an annual Arts Week now for a number of years.]

I'm told this was 'a Rip van Winkle town' in the 1940s and '50s; then things began to change. An important figure in this connection was Hedli MacNeice, widow of the poet, who opened the Spinnaker in 1960 and started a vogue for *fruits de mer*. The Spaniard, up the road, must be the most popular pub on the south coast. Blue murder during the holiday months, it reverts in winter to its original function as a shelter for fishermen, with oilskins steaming round an open fire beneath sepia photographs of ancient mariners. Here, as elsewhere in town, a lively symbiosis has been established between the locals, quiet men with pints, and the multinational crowd of bronzed chaps in fancy sweaters and fast dames with parasols in their drinks. Not that we need much shelter down this way. When rain is general all over Ireland, the sun is shining on Kinsale; and certainly winter is remarkably mild, with the flowers planted for the Tidy Towns Competition refusing to wither and die. I have to go carefully now, since I live here and friends are involved; but I must admit to being a bit dubious about Tidy Towns. Beckett said it long ago: 'What constitutes the charm of our country, apart of course from its scant population, is that all is derelict.' Anachronism; but I too harbour a predilection for Squalid Towns, like the well-known RTÉ personality who, after his first visit to New York, declared it 'a grand big dirty sexy town, not unlike Clonmel'. Still, there's no denying the enhanced civic pride, evident even in the unaccustomed alertness of the municipal drunks who doze, Mexican fashion, in the winter sun outside the Temperance Hall. A Rip van Winkle town no longer, Kinsale even in winter is active and gregarious. It can boast intellectual distinction too, and not just because Elizabeth Bowen and Molly Keane used to meet here for lunch. There are several writers currently in residence, most recently [anachronism] Ireland's premier prose stylist Aidan Higgins. But I realize I've made a great mistake in writing this piece at all, since it will only encourage you lot to jump in your Porsches and come tearing down here in search of a little real estate, waking us up and raising the price of everything. So I take it all back: besides, there's nothing left. You couldn't find a house here for love nor money, certainly not for money. Don't waste your time and our precious parking space. Timoleague, now, there's a tidy town for you.

Kinsale at Work

Contributor: Martin Shanahan and his wife Marie, own and run Fishy Fishy Restaurant, famous for fresh local seafood served in a relaxed atmosphere. Since 2009 Martin has pursued a parallel career as a TV chef and author of cookery books, specialising in seafood, and won many awards. He is known as a great supporter of the local fishing community, whose photographs adorn the walls of his restaurant.

I left Fermoy at 17 and trained as a chef at Rockwell College. I came to Jim Edwards in 1983 to become chef. I was 21 or 22. Probably looking back I was a bit too young for so much responsibility. I came to Kinsale, and I met Marie my wife, she's from Cork City, and we got married here, and really Kinsale has been home ever since. In January 1988 we left Kinsale to go to San Francisco, we worked there until 1991, it was a great time, the food culture around Sausalito and the Bay area was very exciting. But our first love was always Kinsale, and we came back in 1991 with the intention of opening a restaurant and went into business with Jim Edwards.

We opened the Kinsale Gourmet Store in Market Square. It caused a bit of curiosity: if we'd called it the Kinsale Fish Shop people would not have come near us back then, but curiosity alone got them in. They wondered what's a gourmet store? It was a fish shop, but it was also a deli where you could get a bottle of wine, a loaf of home-baked brown bread, you could get a lemon, or you could eat a plate of oysters. We also did outside catering, and added-value products, things like ready-prepared fish pies. We tried to make seafood easy and convenient for people. You could buy the fish, and put it straight into the oven, all the preparation was done for you, and that was a new thing back then. 'No skin, no bone, no fear' to this day that is our mantra. We spent seven years there, then we moved up to a bigger place opposite St Multose, and it was more of a restaurant then a shop. As Irish people travelled more, they got more adventurous and enthusiastic about fish, and sales of seafood grew enormously. And now we have this place in the town park that used to be an art gallery.

From the initial time coming to Kinsale in 1984, I loved it. I remember one night, I wasn't here long, going to the Folk House to a card drive in the middle of the winter, and getting a lock-in until 5 am, which was of its time, then spending another two hours walking round the windy streets trying to find my flat, where I was living at the time. Those streets haven't changed, they stayed small and windy and colourful, and to me that's beautiful. In summertime we have a lot of tourists, sure, but all year round we have visitors. A tourist to me is someone living four or five miles out the road, Belgooly or Ballinspittle or Riverstick, not necessarily from overseas.

My impression of Kinsale, having lived here full time for the last 28 years, and on and off for up to 35 years, is that it has a lovely relaxed feel about it, a holiday feel about it. It's a working town, but it's not an obvious working town. No matter what day of the week you come in, it has a holiday atmosphere. People smile at you in the street, and they're happy. That's driven by tourism. Every facet of this town and every job in this town is associated with tourism to some extent – taxis, pubs, dry cleaners, food, newsagents, cafes – it keeps us going. There's a great pride around the town and I love it. It's a very simple pride, you hear people walking along the street talking about what's going on up at the Pier Head or where ever, with great excitement, there's a great friendship here, and pride in place.

We have three children, the boys are 23 and 21, and Lucy is 16. They're like all Kinsale kids, they're outgoing, because they're used to dealing with people, through the service industry. I see that not just in my kids, but in all the young adults from the town that come to work here, they have this kind of quiet confidence, and that's a skill in itself, you get it quite naturally just living here.

Any time of the year, but definitely more so in the autumn and the winter, you might sneak up to the Spaniard for a couple of pints, and you forget to come home. You drive over to the Bulman and you collect your car three days later. We enjoy the town, it's not just for the visitors, it's for us all, whether it's Monday night or Sunday, there's always a bit of life somewhere.

And the sea, being so close to the sea is a huge influence on us as people, the way it always changes, it's blue, it's green, it's high tide, low tide, storms or calm, it's always changing. And you know, that first glimpse of Kinsale when you're coming down the road from Cork, and you see the town across the water, it makes you feel at home.

Contributor: Jerome Lordan's family has lived at the Old Head of Kinsale for generations. He worked as a commercial fisherman for 28 years and has been the owner of Kinsale Harbour Cruises since 2003. In 2012 he was awarded an M.A. in Local History with First Class Honours for his thesis on the local place names of the Old Head. His book about the shipwrecks of Kinsale and Courtmacsherry, <u>No Flowers on a Sailor's Grave</u> *was published in 2014. [In conversation with AH]*

'I've a historical perspective on Kinsale, I'm very interested in the fishing in Kinsale in the 19th century. It was a fishing town, and during a boom everyone made money, then it went bust, and became very run down. It was a total contrast to today. It's become gentrified, it's like a suburb of Cork nowadays, we've none of the characters that were here in the old days, the old men who'd worked on boats of one sort or another all their lives.

I'm originally from the Old Head which is another parish. When you go over that bridge there's a big change, into the west Cork mindset. I have that fierce loyalty of pride of place, coming from the Old Head.

When people say to me you're from Kinsale, I say I'm not, I'm from the Old Head. It's a huge difference, it's very tribal and it's very Irish, it's a deep-rooted thing. To me the west is familiar, I'd know that whole coast very well, Rosscarbery, Clonakilty, and south Kerry I'd know faces from being a fisherman for years. The coastal people have a different perspective.

So when I drive in to Kinsale I'm very much going to work. I run the boat (Kinsale Harbour Cruises) from March to October, and July and August are very much the peak times. I could go out nine or ten times some days, with private groups as well as the scheduled trips. We have a lot of private bookings. It's quite intensive, and I have help, I couldn't do without it.

I'm kind of immune to the charms of the harbour by now, the same routine every day. People often say to me out in the boat, men in particular, you've the best job in the world on a sunny day, going around the harbour. Actually, it's not, it's very stressful, you've got people in a group who are drunk, a lot of kids aboard the boat, a big tide, or a rope in the propeller, you're just a step away from catastrophe all the time. And you're totally dependent on the weather: when the weather is good you're doing well, and when it's not, you're not. I see people coming down from Cork, and they hop on their yachts, and when they pull out from the marina they are totally relaxed. I'm the opposite, when I tie the boat up and get back on shore, then I'm relaxed. My idea of heaven is going hill walking down on Sheep's Head or Beara or up in the Reeks on *terra firma* instead of going out on the water. When you work on the water all your life it's very hard to associate it with leisure. I remember when I packed up commercial fishing it was about seven years till I went out on a boat for pleasure. It's a very different perspective.'

Contributor: Brian Cronin and his wife Anne were founder members of the Kinsale Good Food Circle as the first owners of the Blue Haven. This is extracted from a speech he gave at the launch of the 40th Kinsale Gourmet Festival in 2017.

I'd like to tell you how it all started: the Kinsale Good Food Circle, the Gourmet Festival itself, and the people who were behind its creation and vision. The unique working-together spirit, the voluntary involvement, and the commitment of individuals have made Kinsale stand out from so many other Irish towns over the past 40 years. Kinsale was a bellwether for what was to follow around the country in tourism, food, and community co-operation.

Kinsale has always punched well above its weight for such a small town. Achieving the title of Ireland's Tidiest Town in 1986, and the European Floral Competition a year later, was a great combination of committed locals from all walks of life, working together with Kinsale Urban District Council. The creation of the International Wine Museum in The French Prison, telling the story of Ireland's 'Wine Geese' families was another exciting development. There are many other examples of events created by creative and committed people which helped to put Kinsale on the map, and I was glad to have played a small role in some of these.

Another outstanding example of somebody who made an exceptional contribution to the town were the two marvellous Guardwell Homes Sheltered Housing schemes which Heide Roche, with the support of her late husband Stanley, and a small local committee brought to fruition.

When Anne and I arrived here with our growing brood in 1972, things were in a pretty gloomy state in the country generally. The Ulster Troubles had decimated our tourism industry, which had always relied heavily on the British and American markets. Ireland was coming out of troubled times as many will remember.

Gerry Galvin arrived the same week as I did: he to manage the Trident Hotel, and me to manage Acton's. The tourism season in Kinsale – such as it was then - extended over six weeks or so, from the June Bank Holiday weekend to the Kinsale Regatta in August. We gathered a few others around us, including Peggy Green who had started a Deep Sea Angling Centre in Kinsale, and we formed an organisation called Kinsale Community Promotions which later became the Kinsale Chamber of Tourism. We roped in the town's three restaurateurs - Hedli MacNiece who started the Spinnaker, and specialised in shellfish, Peter Barry who started the Man Friday and decided to concentrate on meat and steak dishes, and the colourful Gino Gaio whose restaurant had a decidedly Italian flavour.

We decided to concentrate on the Irish market with a series of fun weekends during April and May. These 'Wild Geese' weekends were highly successful, and part of the weekend programmes included dining out at the restaurant of one's choice. We soon realised that working *together*, promoting Kinsale first and foremost, and then promoting each other's restaurants, was a very successful recipe for success. Gerry Galvin and his wife Marie started the Vintage Restaurant, I took over the Blue Haven, Pat Murphy started the White Lady Inn, and now we were six! Lars and Birgitta Safflund started their Bacchus with a decidedly Swedish flavour, and were soon followed by Heide Roche with her stylish Bistro restaurant, whose chef Michael Riese added some decidedly Germanic touches to his menus. Each of these eight restaurants had distinctively different styles of food and atmosphere, but what they all shared in common was a commitment to raise the standards of food and service to as high a level as possible, while simultaneously promoting Kinsale as a Gourmet Centre. Using local fresh produce and ingredients in season, whether meat, fish, vegetables or herbs was also very important. Recommending what you might think were 'competing' restaurants, was a completely new concept and one of the features that made Kinsale distinctively different.

In those early days many new ideas were tried out with varying degrees of success. One of the better ideas was for us to invite a Food Inspector, selected by a contact in the Irish Tourist Board, to visit each restaurant in turn in an anonymous capacity and then to deliver a detailed report of their experience to the restaurant concerned. These reports turned out to be invaluable and a learning curve for all of us. The reviews we routinely give these days on TripAdvisor, for every service we experience, were a long way away from the standards of the early 1970's.

Others who joined our group leading up to that first Gourmet Festival in 1977 were the late Dick Burmby of the Monastery Hotel, and local lads Kieran and Tony Greenway with Skippers Restaurant. So now we had ten! Others who joined that initial group were Jim and Paula Edwards, Wendy Tisdall of Max's Wine Bar, Michael and Rose Frawley of the White House, Philip and Joss Horgan of the Man Friday, Michael Buckley with his Cottage Loft, Michael Riese with the Vintage (MARK-2), Jean Marc, Bernard Hurley with Bernard's, Peter and Fionnuala Jordan of Seasons, Denis and Geraldine Kieran of Shrimps, Carol Norman of Crackpots, and indeed many others - and I'm not even mentioning other members of the present Good Food Circle.

We have had our fair share of dramas. That first Gourmet Festival was a great test of stamina for all of us; having to run a festival and then to have to dash back to our individual restaurants to prove that the proof of the pudding lies in the eating. Many of our guests that weekend were invitees and included members of the press and journalistic world. Disaster nearly struck on the final night when a member of the *Garda Siochana* (not from the local force I might add) pointed out that we didn't have a licence extension, as our Saturday had now become Sunday and we would have to clear our Festival Club forthwith. We came up with a very Irish solution to an Irish problem and having put the word around to all our VIP guests and we all quietly repaired to the Blue Haven Hotel. One of our guests that night was the late Hugh Leonard who wrote about the affair in vivid detail on the following weekend's Sunday Independent. He finished his article by mentioning that a member of the local Gardai tapped on the bar window and suggested that we should keep the noise down as the sing-song was keeping the neighbours awake!

Contributor: Adrian Wistreich is a psychology graduate who spent his career as a research analyst in London, before leaving corporate life in 2000 to start a pottery and arts centre in Kinsale. The pottery has grown to become the largest private craft teaching centre of its kind in the country. Adrian participated in creative writing programmes for many years, and in 2004, was one of the winners of the Fish International Flash Fiction competition. In 2015/16 he studied for the UCC MA in creative writing, and has since written three novels. He is on the organising committee of Words By Water and the management committee of Kinsale Chamber of Tourism.

Pam at the Pottery

I'd arrived in Kinsale and decided to start a pottery school, because I'd loved attending one in North London, and it seemed appropriate to my change of life from corporate businessman to artist. The school opened with a flourish and in typical Kinsale fashion, everyone came for a class or a course to try it out and say they'd been.

Some people came looking for something more. Perhaps it was a sense of themselves, re-connecting with their lost past in creative ways, finding an independence and confidence which some life experience had taken away, or finding solace in something soothing, away from stressful lives in pharmaceutical companies or the like. For some it was a place to re-engage with other Kinsalers who were also lonely.

In the first year, there were five weekly classes, and the morning crowd differed markedly from those who chose to come from work in the evenings. The i-Pod had different playlists for the two sessions.

Eighteen years later, and the local students are far outnumbered by tourists and overseas potters coming to enjoy a course, but across that time there have been many stayers. I have students who've been here for ten years, rarely missing a term, and who see pottery as part of their way of life. Children who came to summer camps at the beginning are bringing their children to summer camps now and attending adult courses themselves. Sadly, there have been several who can no longer come.

Keeping the fire lit, literally and metaphorically, has been hard for me at times, as someone who gets bored and impatient easily, always looking for the next big thing. But the pottery has been an anchor, and Kinsale has been its bedrock. The place is deeply rooted, having been built in 1770 as the coachman's house and stables for Ballinacurra House. There've been only 7 families living here since it was built, before we blew in. I have never lived in one place as long, having moved around a lot over the years, and now it's increasingly hard to envisage moving away.

Pam Jermyn (R.I.P.)

Pam Jermyn, my oldest and longest-standing student, died a couple of years ago at 90. Born in England, she'd lived in Kinsale since the fifties, having met an Irishman who fought in the British army. She was working in GCHQ Cheltenham at the time and he was a commando. They settled in Kinsale after the war, had four children and kept donkeys, teaching local children, now parents, to ride. They both painted scenes from nature and enjoyed annual painting holidays to the West Indies. Pam always wanted to talk about her beloved husband, John, whom she called 'Paddy', who died months before she joined my classes.

I wrote about her some years ago, when I was having doubts about continuing with the pottery:

'Pam arrives with her newly acquired Zimmer frame, chauffeured by her daughter in the familiar ageing Golf. She sets her good leg on the gravel in the crisp sunshine of our first spring day, and levers her body to near vertical, her centre of gravity somewhere between her legs and the frame. She greets me in her precise Queen's English, despite 45 years in Ireland, grips her handbag and tools firmly, and shuffles towards the pottery door. She is still alive, still a force in her surroundings. Her fine white hair is set and her lipstick just so, a statement of the greatest importance.

'She exudes the joy she feels at finally being able to leave the bungalow to return to her class, after her spell in the geriatric ward, and MRSA which nearly carried her off. Nine years without fail she's been coming to the Thursday morning workshop, the longest standing student, always seated in the most comfortable chair by the heater. And as she settles into her new project – an elephant – her life rolls away behind her, hills in shades of green and brown, rich valleys and streams, the war, marriage, careers, children, grandchildren, accolades and achievements all woven into her regal train.

To the others, it's just a morning class, but for Pam it's a statement of vitality, a measure of existence. She's sculpted cats and dogs, stallions and donkeys, portraits of the family, gifts and treasures, struggling to make best use of her arthritic fingers and fading concentration. But in each small piece is a gift of her life-force, an attachment which holds her from her inevitable end.'

I sometimes question whether I have run my course with teaching, but then I think of Pam, and I have no need to question why I do this.

Contributor: One half of the internationally successful fashion label, 'Charlotte and Jane', Charlotte Cargin owes her presence in Kinsale to her grandparents' decision to move here back in the 1960s.

Charlotte Cargin

My grandparents William and Emily Fitzgerald moved to Kinsale with their six young children, my mother being the second, in the 1960s, and my grandfather who was a doctor, became one of the town's two GPs. They were drawn to the beauty of the landscape and chose this town as a place to raise their children and live out their lives. What a blessing this would be for me, though my arrival on the scene was not until the 1980s! They bought The Grove, a charming old Georgian ruin on Compass Hill in what was then a quiet town. It was such a ruin that the bathroom had no roof, and baths had to be taken with the bather holding an umbrella over themselves for privacy. Cows regularly wandered down from the field behind into the house, as the boundary walls had crumbled. The house was a labour of love for my grandparents for the course of their lifetimes and the gardens too.

My grandfather was a passionate and knowledgeable gardener, and he landscaped the sloping land with carefully thought-out terracing, and stunning planting schemes, adding to the collection of shrubs and trees over the years. He always told his children that it would be they, as older adults, and their children and grandchildren who would benefit from the mature gardens that he was creating. Though he would never see his granddaughter living here now with her children, we certainly appreciate all he did in creating this house and garden. It has shaped my life hugely and continues to do so. I'm so grateful they moved here, and that this enchanting town is therefore my home, and that my family is part of this wonderful community.

I moved to London to study fashion design at Central Saint Martin's College of Art and Design, and upon graduating, I moved back to Kinsale where my heart I knew beat strongest. I was determined to set up my own clothing design label, working ethically, producing locally, with natural and locally-sourced fabrics. I wanted to work at a high-end, couture level, making bespoke clothing for women. I wanted to work in a direct, personal way with the clients, the dress-makers and the fabric creators.

By great serendipity soon after my return to Kinsale, Jane Skovgaard, a vibrant Zimbabwean artist, who had been an inspiring and influential teacher to me at the Kinsale College of Further Education before I went to study in London, asked me to design and make her wedding dress. Little did either of us know what a significant moment that was for us both, as there began our collaboration, each inspiring the other and enjoying creating together hugely. We decided to start a dress design label. Jane had a wealth of experience working with textiles and designing them which complemented my experience in tailoring and design. We have taught each other so much during our ten years in business together. We continue daily to draw inspiration from each other, and to help ideas unfold within each other. It is a gift in every way to have a co-creative business partnership.

'Charlotte and Jane', our label, has gone from strength to strength. Our studio is in my grandfather's former workshop space in an old coach house building. When we started out, it was filled with old windows, an old motor bike, all the garden tools, the lawn mower etc! Over those early years we transformed it dramatically, so that it is now our vibrant creative hub. Women travel to meet us from all over Ireland, and even further afield, and we spend time with each of them, trying on sample template designs, of which we have over seventy made up in different sizes. From there we adapt to create just the right design for each client's personality, figure and occasion. We then select which colour and fabric to make the garment in, choosing from our beautiful range at the studio. We have built up a wealth of stunning fabrics, working closely with the producers. In some cases, such as with Kerry Woollen Mills, we design weaves and colourways of bespoke 'Charlotte and Jane' tweeds and wool fabrics. We make the patterns on our enormous table here at the studio, which was my aunt's art restoration table once upon a time, and then the garments are made up by our brilliant dress makers, who work from their homes in the surrounding area.

We started our business with passion, determination, hard work, and of course talent, in mid-recession and now it flourishes. The community of Kinsale has been an enormous support throughout the journey, with the local shop 'Granny's Bottom Drawer' helping us to launch our first collection. The Irish media has been hugely supportive too, with national newspapers featuring our label over the years, and putting us on the front cover of their magazines. We have been on television on *Nationwide*, and featured in the hit series 'Frock Finders' on RTE. With the support of our families, the local community, and the all-important word of mouth, we have established ourselves firmly on the Irish and international fashion scene. It all happens from a former tool shed at my grandparents' former home in Kinsale.

Kinsale is an ideal base for our business, as clients enjoy travelling to meet with us here, and they make an occasion of it, enjoying what the town has to offer. We love the town so deeply, it inspires us daily, and we are delighted to contribute to the mix, and be a part of the wealth of vibrant creative people in this vibrant, creative town.

Contributor: Barry Moloney, a native of Kinsale, is one half of Don and Barry's Historic Stroll in Old Kinsale. He is known for his enthusiasm for Kinsale's history. He also guides for Rick Steves' European tours and others, and has a special interest in Irish writers.

These historical figures who have passed through Kinsale inspire me as I guide historical tours in their footsteps;

Archduke Ferdinand, Cosmo De Medici, Oliver Cromwell, King James II, John & Charles Wesley, Alexander Selkirk, William Dampier, Don Juan Del Aquila, Lord Mountjoy, William Penn, Sir Walter Raleigh, Hugh O'Neill, Red Hugh O'Donnell, Alfred Vanderbilt I, Sir Hugh Lane, Sir Francis Drake, Grace O'Malley, Mary Robinson, Aidan Higgins, Elizabeth Southwell, Anne Bonney, Roy Keane, Sonia O'Sullivan.

Historical figures who have passed through Kinsale

Kinsale Community

Contributor: Malcolm Hall: I was born in the UK but I spent most of my career overseas working in 14 different countries including exotic places such as Swaziland, Ethiopia and Yemen - all of which had certain attractions. However, on my retirement, I chose to spend the rest of my life in Kinsale - a place I first visited on holiday in 2003. Now I have the time to write about my life and travels and about the place I love so much.

Kinsale Men's Shed

Although Kinsale Men's Shed has only been in existence for three years, it is already firmly established as part of the infrastructure of Kinsale, contributing to the well-being of the community.

Kinsale Men's Shed is part of an international organisation known as the Men's Shed movement. This is the definition of a Men's Shed:

'A Men's Shed is a dedicated, friendly and welcoming meeting place where men come together and undertake a variety of mutually agreed activities. Men's Sheds are open to all men regardless of age, background or ability. It is a place where you can share your skills and knowledge with others, learn new skills or redevelop your old skills. New members are always welcome and can be assured that there is something of interest for everyone as the men have ownership of the projects and decide their own programme of events. Objectives of Men's Sheds include advancing the health and well-being of the participating men and contributing to their local communities'.

The movement can be traced back to a conference concerned with the health of men in Australia in 1995. It quickly became apparent that Men's Sheds improved the well-being of people who attended. Here in Ireland, and the government and the HSE support the Men's Shed movement.

There are now over 400 Men's Sheds in Ireland, which is the highest concentration in the world. In January 2015 a committee of Simon Toussifar, Bernard O'Donovan and Dennis Collins began promoting Kinsale Men's Shed (KMS), seeking grants and donations, organising fund-raisers and appealing for premises. In February an open meeting in the Temperance Hall attracted some 34 prospective members. Next month the committee was expanded to include Peter Tiernan, Pat Morrissey, Sean Lynch, Bernard Greaves and Tom Quigley. A profound debt of gratitude is due to these eight founder members. In April 2105 Malcolm Hall joined the committee and serves as the secretary.

Kinsale Men's Shed moved into the loft of Acton's warehouse at the head of the Glen in June 2015. We modified the premises to our needs by building a toilet, tea kitchen and wheelchair friendly access. Special thanks are due to the owner of this property for allowing us to use it. Soon a wood workshop was in production with donated tools and equipment. The KMS membership increased to 40, and the financial turnover was over €8,000 in 2016. KMS is not a commercial concern, but income is derived from the sale of goods made in the workshop, sales of a calendar, hosting presentations, grants and membership fees, as well as generous donations from individuals, businesses and local organisations.

KMS provides a relaxed venue where men, can meet for social engagement, activities and pastimes. Most of the activities are in some way a service to the community. Products from our workshop have aided local schools, the community hospital, churches, local artists, KYCC, KYSS, theatre groups, the St Patrick Day Parade, the community orchard project and individual members. We have held many social gatherings with talks to the public on topics including history, healthy living and travel. Regular weekly sessions include metal and wood workshops, yoga, choir, card games, creative writing and ukulele practice. The Shed has held training courses, for members and non-members, in the making of *sugan* stools and woodturning. Several new members have been referred to KMS by both private and HSE health practitioners. Ever keen to take on new challenges, KMS will be launching a book of short stories and poetry written by members at *Words by Water*, Kinsale Literary Festival, 2018.

Kinsale Men's Shed welcomes new members, young and old, from all walks of life and with all skill levels. Learn something new and interesting or share your skills with others. It is our aim to do further service to the community and grow in stature by contributing to the well-being of Kinsale.

Contributor: Elizabeth Creed has lived in Kinsale with her family since 2003, and joined Transition Town Kinsale in 2006. Over the years she has been involved with initiatives across all the working groups, food, energy, transport, waste reduction and community awareness.

Transition Town Kinsale - a Short History

Vision without action is merely a dream

Action without vision only passes the time

Vision with action can change the world.

Joel Barker

When Transition Town Kinsale (TTK) marked its tenth Birthday in 2015, we celebrated the work of the volunteers and supporters who helped keep the initiative alive by creating conversations in our community about how to secure a brighter sustainable future for all. Our vision is a thriving "low-carbon" town, and a resilient, inclusive community.

In 2005, Louise Rooney and Catherine Dunne, students at Kinsale College, adopted the Kinsale Energy Descent Action Plan

(KEDAP), and started promoting and creating a resilient, sustainable community which they named Transition Town Kinsale. KEDAP began as a project undertaken by Permaculture Course participants under the direction of Rob Hopkins, who went on to spearhead Transition in Totnes, England. In Kinsale, the Town Council agreed to support this fledgling organisation with funding, and now TKK is one of a thousand Transition initiatives in over 50 countries.

TTK 10th Birthday Celebrations 2015

Over the past 13 years we have worked with many community and business groups including Tidy Towns, the Chamber of Tourism, the Good Food Circle; Kinsale Arts Week (now Weekend); local primary and post-primary schools, Kinsale College; Sáile; Foróige, Kinsale Active Retirement Association, and more recently The Men's Shed, Plastic Free Kinsale and Kinsale Tennis Club. Our steering committee is the glue which holds this unique community organisation together, creating links and enabling pop-up groups to facilitate projects.

In addition to our own fund-raising efforts we have received support from Cork County Council, Kinsale Town Council, Local Agenda 21, West Cork Development Partnership, Léargas, Kinsale Credit Union, Kinsale Lions Club, RX3, the AIB and others. Our most ambitious project to date was a feasibility study for a local anaerobic digestor. We have run numerous Open Space events, inviting all in the community to visualise what Kinsale could look like in a low-carbon future. We also run many fun family events to raise green-awareness.

Earthhour in Kinsale 2011

We have hosted workshops by experts in biodiversity, ecology and food foraging and organised Open Forum and film events to discuss topics such as 'Can Kinsale feed itself', and 'The Future of Money'. We have celebrated Earth Hour and supported Cork Climate Action and national lobby groups such as Stop Climate Chaos.

In the early days we had a community garden at Sean Hales Terrace, and now our Edible Landscaping Trail is on Kinsale maps. We planted fruit and nut trees in the newer housing estates, and in 2010 we began planting Kinsale's Community Orchard in partnership with the Sáile Committee and Kinsale College. We are now reaping the harvest in this community space.

Meitheal at the Community Orchard 2018

TTK has worked with local primary schools in developing their school gardens and we have also organised sow & grow workshops. To promote local food production, we developed the 50 Mile Meal Award, launched at the Kinsale Gourmet Festival in 2007. The award can now be found on restaurant and café menus in town. The 50 Mile Award is used in local shops to highlight products grown or produced in Cork. Through our Community Supported Agriculture scheme we have worked with local farmers to grow oats and quinoa, and to buy produce directly (vegetables, eggs, chickens and honey).

In 2009, TTK made a submission to the Kinsale Traffic Management Plan and have since campaigned for its implementation. We liaised with West Cork Rural Transport to develop a better local transport system and welcome the new improved local-link service. We continue to campaign for better public transport, and the promotion and development of walkways and cycleways around Kinsale.

TTK Food Forage Walk at Charles Fort

We have worked with Tidy Towns over the years during the annual An Taisce Spring Clean. In 2018, working with Plastic Free Kinsale and Tidy Towns, we have begun a 'Reducing our Waste' initiative with the 'Voice Recycling' and 'Stop Food Waste' workshops.

We have supported local businesses through our 50 Mile Award and supported the establishment of the Farmers' Market, the Ringrone Allotments and a Community-Supported Agriculture scheme. In 2018 we set up Kinsale Community Energy Project (KCEP). As the birthplace of the Transition Movement we have raised Kinsale's profile and have had many "Transition visitors" over the years from every corner of the world.

Launch 50 Mile Award (shops & restaurants) 2012

It is difficult to quantify our achievements, but at the very least we have started conversations in our community which will enable us to take on the challenge of creating our low carbon future. It is important for our community to meet this challenge, not only because of Ireland's commitments under the Paris Agreement but because of our responsibility as global citizens.

TTK has endeavoured to be both a catalyst for climate change action locally, and a catalyst for action nationally by lobbying decision makers. TTK believes that we need to do things differently to make the necessary transition and this has been reflected in the submissions we have made to our Local Area Development Plan and others.

Our Transition journey in Kinsale has been about people in our community caring for others, and for the environment. Our "just transition" approach demands climate action now, with the benefits and costs of climate change action being shared in an equitable way locally and globally.

Green Day at Kinsale Arts Week 2011

Contributor: Paul Eaton was the last person to be employed as porter by the Allied Irish Bank, Kinsale. Before that he was a familiar face in the newsagents Boland's and Favourites. His family are raise funds and regularly participapte in the Kinsale Parish pilgrimage to Lourdes. [Audio recording by Aine Wade]

My mother was Hurley, my grandfather used to have a pony and trap delivering things around for people, almost like what you would do in a van now: he would collect things for people and drop things off for people. Mam was from a family of nine, and then my father came to work in Kinsale and met Mam, and I am the baby of thirteen. Of all of us born and reared here in Kinsale, the only person who is not here is my brother but he only lives down the road in Midleton.

You know how people always go away and make their homes in different places? Well, we never had that in Kinsale. I don't know there was just that beautiful bond in Kinsale – the whole place , the people , everybody knows everyone and people are very welcoming to everyone, and we have that beautiful community spirit. I could never say we have lost that Kinsale, the spirit is still there. People I've spoken to as I have been involved in the community tell me that the people of Kinsale are very welcoming, and they don't get that same feeling in other parts of the country. I think you have to come to Kinsale and live here for a while to experience it. People who have come from abroad say they love the countryside and the people.

Kinsale is steeped in history, but it being a garrison town, that never comes up, it's been forgotten. People will tell you, when you go away and say you live in Kinsale, they say 'Oh, the Gourmet Capital of Ireland'. I met two people when I worked in the bank and they were telling me they were leaving Kinsale and they were heartbroken as they were getting older and needed to be nearer family. You know they are only one couple but people are heartbroken if they have to leave here.

Kinsale has that thing of adopting you when you come in. Everybody says hallo to people, so people have a sense of belonging.

I have a big worry that the community will not be able to hold on their people, as they cannot afford to live here. More and more wealthy people will come here and buy up the place. They need to mind and nourish the people that are here. We have out-priced ourselves. The children of friends of mine have moved out to buy houses, but they are always keeping an eye out for somewhere in Kinsale.

The special thing about Kinsale is that sense of community and I hope we don't lose that. We have beauty all round us. Kinsale has everything. It is magical.

Contributor: Christina Broderick lives in Kinsale and is a qualified teacher. She has published two books of poetry which can be found in Kinsale's bookshops.

Kinsale

1

Kinsale is a wonderful town

Located in the south of County Cork

I'm glad to have grown up there

About the town I really care

2

Kinsale is a touristy place

Especially during the summer months

But the locals make the town the best

To have them all we're truly blessed

3

Kinsale is a unique spot

It's got many special attractions

It's got loads of amenities

And beautiful views surrounded by seas

4

Kinsale is an ideal destination

For people from near and far

It's got good shops, restaurants and bars

But sometimes it has too many cars

5

Kinsale is where I call home

It's a place special to me

With friends, family and local folk

Kinsale town is no joke!

Contributor: Dearbhail Connon is a visual artist, film maker, art psychotherapist and Shamanic practitioner. She moved to West Cork almost 20 years ago and has been living in Kinsale for 12 years. She moved to Kinsale when her son Leon was 8. He attended Summercove National School and Kinsale Community School. A keen sportsman, with a love of all things traditionally Irish he is best remembered for his warmth and friendship. He knew how to make everyone laugh and smile. He loved Kinsale and the relative safety, freedom and beauty it offers to children and young people growing up.

In memory of Leon

I came to Kinsale roughly eleven years ago. I have witnessed its ongoing transition. The world is in a huge transition right now. Change is relentless and the only surety. We have just undergone both the coldest winter and the hottest summer. I arrived in Kinsale, a relative stranger, roughly eleven years ago with my son Leon. He has since passed away. The Town Council granted me permission to plant a tree and place a bench in his honour near 'the bridge' in Kinsale. This gesture of kindness I do not take lightly. It has become a place of peace and tranquillity for many including myself. It has been said in time it may become known as Leon's Place. I hope so. It is a gesture of love and how the memory of those we have loved lives on through us. It is also a nod to the youth, and how they carry our brightest hope into the future.

Contributor: Alannah Hopkin (See Introduction)

    In 1987 I was living on the top floor of the Dutch House in Cork Street with my husband Aidan Higgins. Wackers was our neighbour down the hill, near O'Brien's fish shop. Aidan got talking to Wackers in the Armada Bar, where he was often given his lunch, and told me the story of Davy and the "silent gun". After the anonymity of central London, I was very touched by the way that Jamesie was quietly looked after within the community. I changed his surname to preserve his privacy.

Wackers

Wackers

Jamesie O'Farrell is soft in the head,
Knows that he's haunted by Davy, who's dead;
Davy comes back in the shape of a crow
And goes for poor Jamesie, flying in low.

The kids call old Jamesie "Wackers" for fun:
'Wackers, hey Wackers, where's the silent gun?'
Jamesie just scowls and walks on as he knows
The silent gun is only for crows.

Catapult aimed at a crow in a tree
Lets fly a stone but the grey crow goes free.
Jamesie staggers, curses, puts it away:
He knows he'll get Davy some other day.

In summer Jamesie is known as "Them Fleas",
'They're out to get me,' he mutters of these
Familiars who buzz in clots round his eyes:
'Them fleas, they is out to get me,' he sighs.

He lives in an old shop called Wacker's Place,
Its window hung with incongruous lace.

In summer sunsets he sits by the door
And lifts a mug of strong tea from the floor.

He will have no electric light inside,
His place is the same as when Davy died;
Davy, he fears, will come back there one day
And tell old Jamesie he must go away.

He cooks and keeps warm by a fire of wood
That he scavenges daily along with some food
That he shares with several local stray cats
Who protect him from Davy, crows and rats.

Jamesie O'Farrell is soft in the head,
Knows that he's haunted by Davy, who's dead;
Davy comes back in the shape of a crow
And goes for poor Jamesie, flying in low.

The kids call old Jamesie "Wackers" for fun:
'Wackers, hey Wackers, where's the silent gun?'
Jamesie just scowls and walks on as he knows
The silent gun is only for crows.

Contributor: Sheila Forde

I am Kinsale

Poised on the Harbour opening my mouth to the river Bandon
Nestling on cliffs and hills with views all the way to the sea.
Of narrow lanes and great big stairs
To precious nooks and crannies.

Grey slates glisten my roofs and clad my walls manifesting
Patina shades of age when rain drops fall.
Like a chameleon changing colour with the changing tides
From mud baths of brown to waters so blue.

The history of my life is there to see in stone and sunken ship graves.
The battle of 1601 leaving my spine exposed
Charles Fort and James Fort my protecting walls
Saving my skeleton from further incursions.

Fishing boats sailing my seas in pursuit of mackerel
Herring and other fruits of the sea with seals in hot pursuit.
Large white sails on elegant yachts,
Cruising in and out every day in sync with the tides.

I am a town of panoramic colour, bustling
So proud to be so unique and oozing with charm.
Magnetising artists, writers and gourmet chefs
Inspiring them to explore and flaunt artistic gifts.

I am Kinsale
You the natives and visitors enriching me to what I am.
I am a facilitator for you to explore and cherish
Paint my picture
And I will brightly shine and provide that glow for you.

Photographs

Summer outside Stone Mad - Debbie Morris

A spectacular sunset from our Boat House balcony in Summercove - Peter Frey

A break from blackberrying, Sandycove - Dave Fannin

Anchor - Teresa O Donnell

Castlepark - Alannah Hopkin

St Multose Church from Market Square, 1986

Market Street, 1984 - Brian Lalor

Stoney Steps - Brian Lalor

The Courthouse, 1984 - Brian Lalor

The Dutch House, Cork Street - Brian Lalor

The French Prison - Brian Lalor

The Bulman in the snow - Harry Dunnican

Putting Up The Christmas Lights 25.11.17 - Alannah Hopkin

After Storm Ophelia - Alannah Hopkin

Charles Fort in Snow 2018 - Teresa O Donnell

Art by water in Kinsale… – Peter Frey

As soon as I stepped off the 226 bus, I knew Kinsale was my forever home – Caoimhe Nace

Hookers - Dermot Ryan

Garretstown Evening - Teresa O Donnell

Compass Hill from the air - Michael Prior

Harbour view - Margaret Waller

Sometimes you forget what's around you, and your surroundings become too familiar to photograph, then you get a still morning like this and you are reminded of the beauty of Kinsale and the place you live in - Giles Norman

From the bridge to World's End at night - Michael Prior

We don't get a lot of snow in Kinsale, so when we do, you have to be early, before the footprints and wheels destroy our seldom-seen snow-covered streets. The snow of '91 eventually melted away, but The Grey Hound still remains today as one of Kinsale's oldest pubs - Giles Norman

Courtney Pine playing at Charles Fort during Kinsale Arts Week

Market Lane reflection - Joachim Beug

The Grey Hound - Tomas Liniecki

Where the sea meets the land, there will always be a canvas for photographers to find, so for me, living in a seaside town is the dream - Giles Norman

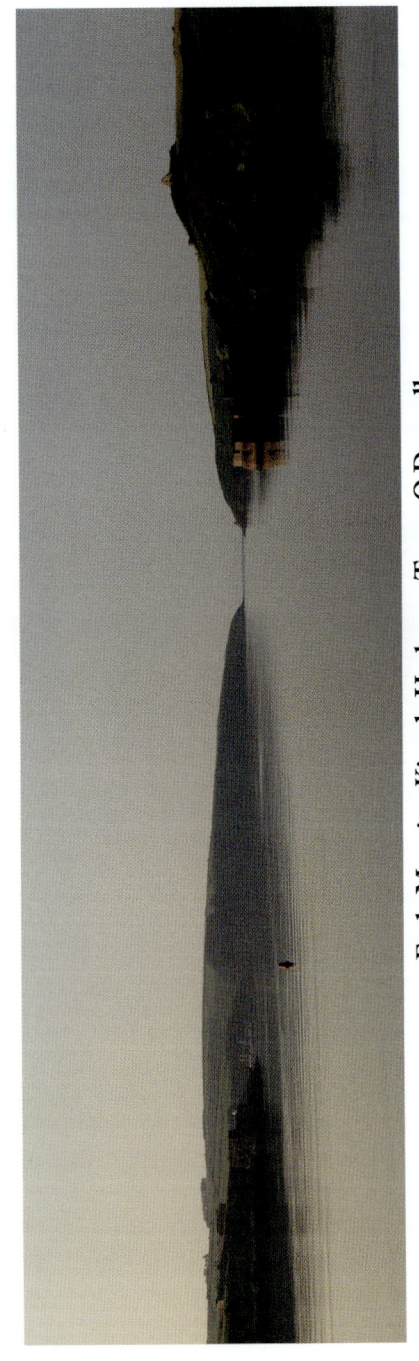

Early Morning Kinsale Harbour - Teresa O Donnell

Kinsale Harbour panorama - Ben O Donnell

This photograph was taken in 1981, the first year of my portfolio, and captures the timeless beauty of Kinsale's harbour, which still lives on today - Giles Norman

Kinsale sunset - Paul Deane

Kinsale winter - Paul Deane

Kinsale Harbour - Conor McCloskey

I mostly photograph the sea from the land, alone on the shore without tiller or sail to worry about, but I took to the sea this day to capture the stunning form of the Asgard, with beautiful Summercove in the background - Giles Norman

Kinsale Summer - Paul Deane

Kinsale Harbour view - Alice Tallent

Out towards the mouth of Kinsale Harbour - Harry Dunnican

Oysterhaven Wreck - Neil Payne

Kinsale Mast - Conor McCloskey

Local - Dave Fannin

Sailing in Kinsale Harbour - Margaret Waller

Once Upon a Starry Night - Michael Prior

Landscape and Bandon River - Adrian Wistreich

Misty morning - Dave Fannin

The Beast from the East - Tomas Linieki

The Lower Road - Pamela Hardesty

Scilly Walk - 1 - Claire Keating

There's nothing quite like a stroll long Kinsale Harbour and a pint at the Bullman! - Caoimhe Nace

Lifeboat - Paul Deane

Rainbow over Worlds End - Adrian Wistreich

Scilly in the Mist - Michael Prior

I've always enjoyed trying to capture the power of raging waves, and with the lighthouse as a backdrop, the Old Head of Kinsale is the perfect spot for this – Giles Norman

Rainbow Harbour - Neil Payne

Sketchbook (3) - de Courcey Country - Katherine Boucher Beug

Sketchbook 01 (9) - Milewater - Katherine Boucher Beug

Sketchbook (11) - Pole Cross - Katherine Boucher Beug

Sketchbook (12) Holly Hill - Katherine Boucher Beug

Sketchbook (14) - The Druids - Katherine Boucher Beug

Sketchbook (15) - Courtaparteen - Katherine Boucher Beug

New Bridge mist - Conor McCloskey

Scilly Walk - 2 - Claire Keating

Sleepy Kinsale - Michael Prior

Sandycove - Dave Fannin

Snow in Charles Fort - Ben O Donnell

Summer rain - Paul Deane

Summer Cove Storm - Tomas Liniecki

Spring Tide at Night - Michael Prior

Waves at The Bulman - Ben O Donnell

Sunset Over Kinsale - Claire Keating

The Mast - Alice Tallent

Morning view across the Bandon River - Adrian Wistreich

Tree moon Dunderrow - Conor McCloskey

View From Ardbrack 1 - Claire Keating

St Patrick's Day Fireworks - Michael Prior

View from Ardbrack - Paul Deane

After the railroad, a different track emerges… - Peter Frey

Scilly Walk - Teresa O Donnell

Stone Mad - Michael Prior

View from The Dock - Adrian Wistreich

An ominous sight at the Kinsale harbor wall...
or was it just a really great date - Peter Frey

The Lower Road - new use for an old pump - Alannah Hopkin

Twilight on Kinsale Marina - Alice Tallent

A time machine comes to Kinsale... - Peter Frey

At the starting line of the Kinsale Grand Prix... - Peter Frey

Painting of The Glen - Norma Mulligan

Mareta Doyle launches Kinsale Arts Week 2006

Arts Week 2006 launch

Awarding Length of Service Medals Kinsale Barracks

Lettice Knolles above old bridge to Kinsale 1910

Bruno's - Paul Deane

Bruno's in the snow - Paul Deane

Stone of Destiny - Dermot Ryan

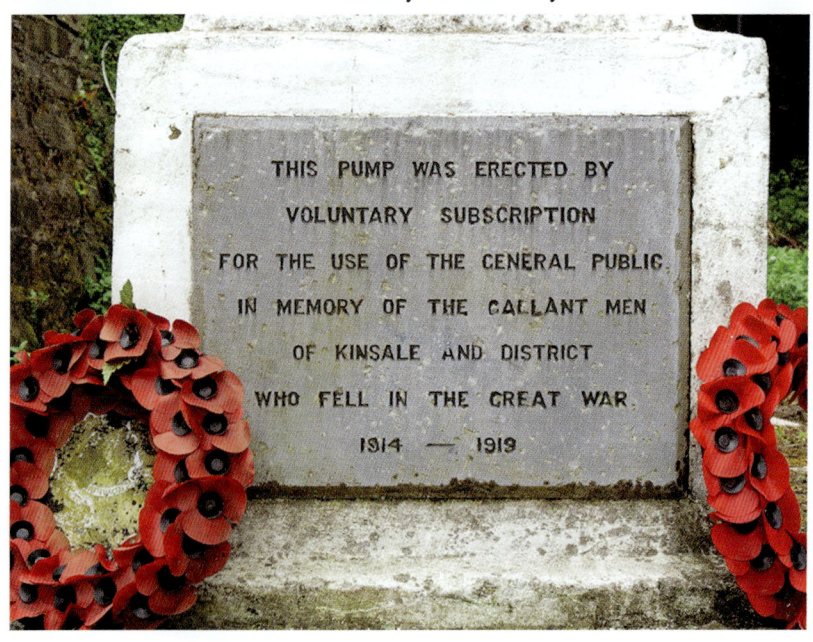

War Memorial, World's End - Dermot Ryan

Kinsale Courthouse - Dermot Ryan

Kinsale Workhouse - Dermot Ryan

Steps down from the Bowling Green - Joachim Beug

Down towards Chairmans Lane - Joachim Beug

Dressing the Parish Church - Joachim Beug

Not even a snowstorm could cancel the
Breast Cancer Walk - Caoimhe Nace

Sunset from Castlepark - Michael Prior

Fishy Fishy philosophy... - Peter Frey

Flowers in Market Place - Joachim Beug

Friary Field - Georgina Sutton

May and June in The Fiary Field - Georgina Sutton

It is the people and families of this town, that make Kinsale wonderful - Caoimhe Nace

Hot Chocolate! - Dave Fannin

Snowy street - Dave Fannin

Snow on The Dock Beach - Aileen Hurley

You see the strangest things in the Supervalu parking lot - Peter Frey

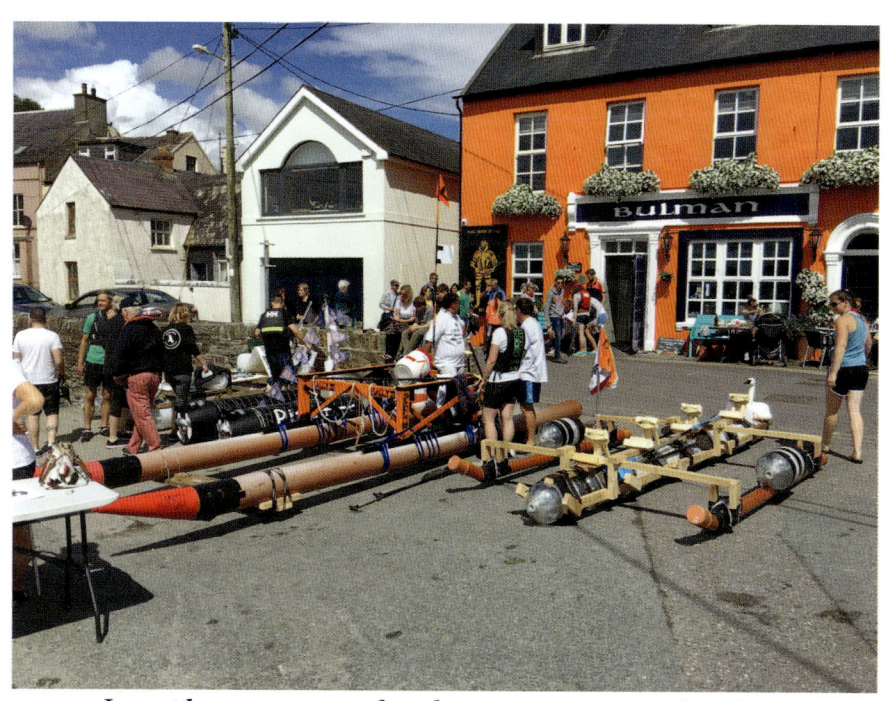

Intrepid seamen prepare for a dangerous crossing... - Peter Frey

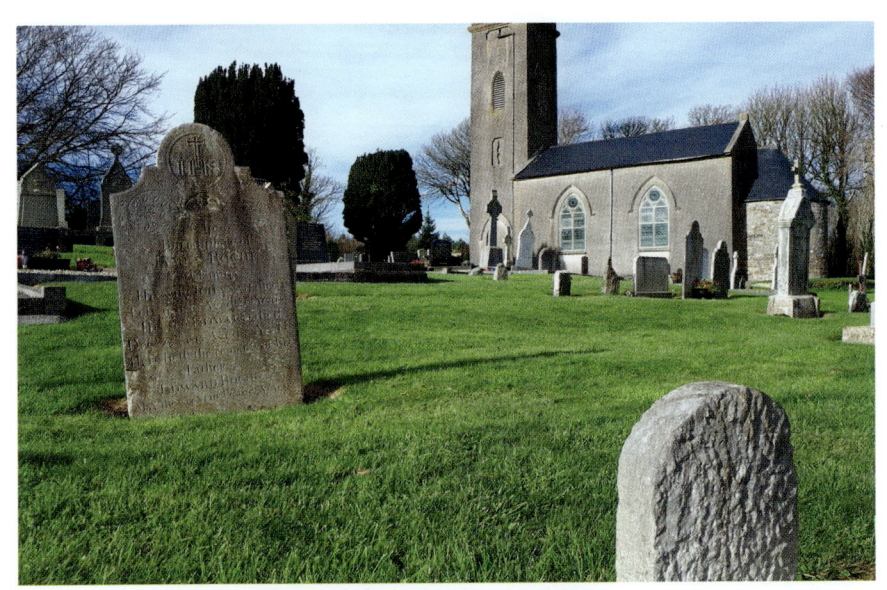

Templetrine Church - Neil Payne

James Fort in the morning sun - Adrian Wistreich

Kinsale Arts Week Installation 2010 - Adrian Wistreich

Kinsale Arts Week installation next morning - Adrian Wistreich

Scilly - Autumn Reflection - Alannah Hopkin

Old Summer Cove

Vintage Postcard

Kinsale Cloaks - Dermot Ryan

Lynch shop in Kinsale

Kinsale Bungalow 1911

Kinsale Sergeants' Sports 1912

Market Lane - Tomas Liniecki

To The Island! (Sandycove) - Alannah Hopkin

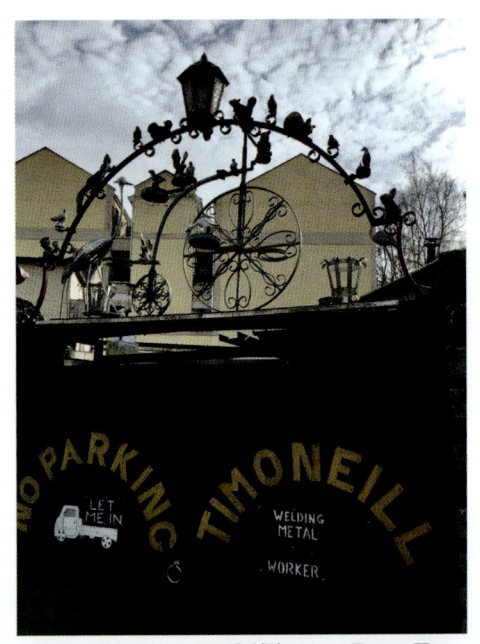

Kinsale's Own Eiffel Tower - Peter Frey

The Garage - Joachim Beug

The Glen - Joachim Beug

The Glen 2 - Joachim Beug

Café terrace at night 2016 - Tomas Liniecki

The Pier - Cathal O'Connor

Garretstown Beach - Neil Payne

Pauper's Well - Neil Payne

The Milky Way over Bolands - Michael Prior

Kinsale in the snow - Paul Deane

Back of the Grey Hound - Joachim Beug

From the Scilly Dam

Sunrise at The Dock - Ben O Donnell

Historical Kinsale

Contributor: John Thuillier's family were boatbuilders for many generations at a site upriver from the Trident Hotel. He wass the founder and is now a retired director of Kinsale Further Education College. He is widely acknowledged as the expert on Kinsale's maritime tradition. He has contributed to many books and journals and has lectured widely on the history of Kinsale. This extract from <u>Kinsale Harbour</u> by John Thuillier (The Collins Press, 2014), is used by kind permission of the author and publisher.

The Place Names of Kinsale Harbour

Crews of visiting ships met the people of the small communities living on the shore around the harbour and witnessed the bare subsistence levels on which they survived. At settlements, south of Charles Fort, people scavenged for a living from the sea and land. Similarly, the community on the Old Head, like the nesting shearwaters on the cliff ledges below, clung for survival, in mud and stone huts attached to the ruined walls of older structures.

Both these areas were Irish speaking where names in Irish were used for the smallest inlets and rock features. In modern times the helms of engine-powered boats rarely need to consider the tide in the harbour. Formerly, small boats, depended on sail and oars, hugged the shore to reduce the effect of a strong counter current. Shelter from a sudden squall, the need for rest and landing places for nets and fish were found in little inlets known as 'cushanna' or, in the lee of rocky outcrops, 'Carraigheanna'. People had an intimate knowledge of the shoreline. They, together with the lobstermen, operating close inshore, became familiar with features and inevitably gave names to places they encountered frequently. Droichead na Fine off Garretstown, as its name, 'the bridge of wine', suggests was the wreck site of a ship spilling its cargo of wine casks into the sea, no doubt to the satisfaction and pleasure of some in the area. Viewed from the north, the Old Head peninsula takes the shape of a corpulent man facing west, supporting a belly-like feature called Cnoc a' Bolg and on the eastern side the other physiognomical extremity, the Tóin (or Bottom) point. Faill an Aifrinn (Mass Rock) is the location where Mass was said in penal times, hidden amid the rocks and close enough to the water for people to escape by boat if discovered by the authorities who had banned the practice of Catholicism. A number of other Mass rocks were located on the eastern side of the harbour itself, at Claidhe an Aifrinn (mass fence) and at Preghane, both locations close to the sea. The practice was noted by Cosimo de Medici, a member of the Florentine banking family, influential in European affairs, when he arrived in Kinsale in 1669 after his ship was blown off course in heavy weather. He was highly critical of the prohibition on religious freedom. The roar of the sea crashing on the rocks is conveyed in the name Faill na nGlór. On a calm day the blueness of the deep water is well described by Cuas Gorm, just west of the tip of the Head. On the eastern side, boats sheltering crept into the corner of Hole Open to boil a kettle, which is appropriately called An Cistin (The Kitchen). Across Bullen's Bay, Cuas Buí with its yellow-coloured sand was popular for bathing. In contrast, reflecting the tragedies that attach to seaboard life is Cuas an Duine Bháite where, in circumstances now forgotten, the remains of a drowned sailor were washed ashore. Further towards Duneen is Oileán Glas – the Green Island – but due to erosion of the soil the grass no longer grows. It was here for security that the explosive powder for the lighthouse fog signal was stored.

Inside the mouth of the harbour itself on the eastern shore, Irish names were prevalent. On the stretch of shoreline from Charles Fort to Ballymaccus Point, women, perhaps washing and drying clothes, gathered at Carraig n Ban (Women's Rock) close to Cuas Lár (Middle Cove). Across the Cove there was Carraig na Rón (rock of the Seal). Cuas Fáinleoga is further south where swallows gather in the autumn for their flight south, and close by in Ceannn Chapill (the Horse's

Head Rock). Cuas Innill – 'safe inlet' – provide security for boats and southwest towards Eastern Point is a blowhole – Poll a'Talaimh' located below the Crooked Ditch, a well-known mark for fishing. Préachán or Prehane, the Crow's Point, comes into view after rounding Eastern Point.

These are a small sample of the names in Irish spoken among the native people outside the town that were common up to the end of the nineteenth century. Ironically, the locations most associated with the use of Irish names were those surrounding British military installations, the garrison at Charles Fort and the coastguard at the Old Head.

Contributor: Fergal Browne is a native of Belgooly, with a keen interest in local history. He has contributed articles relating to the history of Belgooly and Kinsale to various historical journals and edited a local history book on the Parish of Clontead, entitled In the Shadow of Sliabh Rua *(2016). He is also the administrator of the Facebook Page 'Photos of Old Kinsale'. He now lives in Monasterevin, Co. Kildare, with his wife Katherine and son Andrew.*

The Kinsale Aristocracy

The playwright, Lennox Robinson, in his memoirs of growing up in Kinsale in the 1890's, *Three Homes,* recalled: 'Country Society was represented by families such as the Heards of Pallastown, the Meades of Ballymartle and Ballintubber, the Knowles [also written Knolles] of Walton Court, the Cramers of Rathmore. These were our aristocracy; they mingled to some extent with the gentry of the town, but only to some extent. The Heards and the Stopfords (who were an offshoot of the Cramers) gave wonderful children's parties in the winter, parties which I looked forward to in an agony of shyness.'

An examination of newspapers from the nineteenth Century shows the extent to which these were the leading families of the town, both politically and socially, while a cursory view of today's newspapers and voting registers indicates how completely they have vanished. The last direct descendant of the Knolles family passed away in South Africa in February 2017, while the descendants of the Meade and Heard families reside in the UK.

The Heard family originated in Cork in 1579 when John Heard, of Wiltshire, arrived in Ireland with Walter Raleigh, and was granted lands in Bandon. In 1834 his descendant, John Isaac Heard purchased the freehold of much of the town of Kinsale from the estate of the late Lord de Clifford. This made him one of the largest landowners in the town. He was also a politician, and such was his influence in the town that he was known as 'King Heard'. In 1864, using profit from the rent of the family's urban properties, John Isaac Heard's son Captain Robert Heard purchased Pallastown House, near Belgooly. While Pallastown became their country seat, with an estate of 2,000 acres, the family had their town-house at No.10 Fisher Street, (now part of Acton's Hotel). In 1897, the entire family property was inherited by a two-year-old boy, Robert Henry Warren Heard. The following year, Robert's mother, Charlotte Heard, married Richard Charles Pratt, who became stepfather to the young heir. The Pratts were another prominent family in Kinsale, though not of 'landed gentry stock'. The new Mr. and Mrs Pratt, together with the four Heard children, moved into the Heard family townhouse.

Robert H.W. Heard was educated privately in England and finished his education just as the First World War was starting. He was commissioned into the Irish Guards Regiment in 1914. During the war he was wounded and invalided home twice. In 1916, while convalescing, he was presented with an illuminated address by prominent citizens of the town at a ceremony at the Court House. As the young heir of a large estate, he had everything to live for. However, he was badly wounded in a gas attack in the last months of the war. He died of pneumonia, complicated by the damage done to his lungs by the gas attack, in March 1919 and is buried in St. Multose Cemetery together with his father and sister. The Heard estate dwindled in the years that followed.

Lieutenant Robert Henry Warren Heard (1895-1919). Heir to the Heard Estates and owner of much of the Freehold of the town of Kinsale

The Heard Family Townhouse – No.10 Fisher Street, Kinsale, now the site of Acton's Hotel. Photo courtesy of Nicholas Cook

Like many of the 'gentry' families of Kinsale, the Knolles family arrived in Ireland during the Cromwellian period of the 17th Century. They were granted 886 acres near Belgooly and named their estate Oatlands as a family tradition held that they were the first to introduce white oats to Ireland. Famous as huntsmen, the Knolles family were also prominent amongst the Kinsale gentry. Captain Thomas Knolles was a member of the Kinsale Knot of Friendly Brothers, a quasi-masonic society in the town, and was commemorated with a plaque in St. Multose Church after he died in 1840. The plaque gives his name as 'Thomas Friendly Knolles', as each member of the club had to take the word 'Friendly' as a middle name.

His son, Thomas Walton Knolles was a magistrate in the town and served as vice-chairman of the Kinsale Board of Guardians, which ran the workhouse. His name appears at every important gathering in the town for most of the 19th Century. His brother Francis inherited Walton Court near Oysterhaven from a cousin; this was the Knolles of Walton Court branch to which Lennox Robinson referred. When Thomas Walton Knolles died in 1890, the Oatlands Estate passed to a cousin, Thomas Hamilton William Knolles, who moved there with his family. In 1905 his daughter Jean was married to Colonel Henry T Manley at St. Multose Church. Thomas H.W. Knolles died in 1913, and is buried in St. Catherine's Church, Ringcurran. The Knolles family sold Oatlands and left the area in 1937.

Monument to Captain Thomas 'Friendly' Knolles in St. Multose Church. Photo courtesy of Carol Newburn

Thomas Walton Knolles (1808-1890), Magistrate of Kinsale, Vice Chairman of Kinsale Board of Guardians and Master of South Union Hunt

Wedding of Jean Knolles to Lt.Col Henry T. Manley which took place at St. Multose Church on 4th July 1905

Unlike other gentry families in the area, the Meade family were an ancient Irish family, originating in the Buttevant area. The family estate was at Ballymartle, near Riverstick. When King James II landed at Kinsale in 1689, Robert Meade of Ballymartle was the first to greet him on the quay, in his role as Sovereign of Kinsale. Despite politically 'backing the wrong horse', the Meade family held on to their estates following James's defeat at the Battle of the Boyne. By the 19th Century the head of the family was William Richard Meade. A qualified barrister, he served as Chairman of the Board of Guardians and was also one of the town's magistrates. He worked hard to alleviate the suffering in the area during the Great Famine. He was also prominent in attempts to bring the railway to the town. His niece, Louisa, who, together with her mother and siblings, lived with him, recalled in her diary of 1884 attending cricket matches and dances at Charles Fort, hosted by the garrison. When William R. Meade died in 1894, his estate was inherited by his nephew, Major Richard John Meade. Major Meade lived at Ballymartle House with his two sisters, but in 1953 he sold the house and moved into Acton's Hotel as a permanent resident. His sister, Dorothea Fowle, lived at Summercove. Major Meade died in 1955.

William Richard Meade (1804-1894), Magistrate of Kinsale, Chairman of Kinsale Board of Guardians. (Image courtesy of William Hall)

The surnames of the Kinsale 'Aristocratic' families exist now solely on the names of a few landmarks – such as 'Heard's Bridge' and in the memories of some of the older residents in the town. They represented an old order now long since swept away.

Contributor: Brian Lalor is one of Ireland's leading graphic artists. He studied at the Crawford School of Art in Cork and worked in architecture and archaeology before moving to west Cork in 1971, where he lived for 14 years. He was chairman of the Graphic Arts Studio in Dublin, and subsequently of Cork Printmakers. He edited <u>Blue Guide Ireland</u> and <u>The Encyclopaedia of Ireland</u> (2003). He is once again living in west Cork and is the Curator of the Ballydehob Arts Museum. This extract from <u>West of West</u> (Brandon 1990) is used with his kind permission.

St Multose Church from Market Square, 1986

Kinsale is one of a small group of Irish country towns with substantial numbers of buildings which date back earlier than the nineteenth century. From the thirteenth-century Saint Multose' church onwards, the town has a rich and interesting selection of houses, public buildings, churches, almshouses and military structures filling out the medieval form of the old town. This plan at once escapes the linear concept and you can lose your way in back lanes and shortcuts, each returning upon itself like the convolutions of a shell. This is the root rather than the node, winding and interlocking and finding itself again.

It is the best point from which to leave or approach West Cork as its architecturally expansive style relates it more to the outside world. Indeed in political terms, the only points of contact between continental Europe and the south-west of Ireland occurred at Kinsale – with the Spanish – and at Bantry – with the French. However, Kinsale is alone in retaining a feeling of that involvement. Its harbour is defended by a star fort designed by Sir William Robinson, whose Royal Hospital at Kilmainham in Dublin was the first important post-medieval building in Ireland. With the Royal Hospital and Charles' Fort in Kinsale, he introduced the spirit of renaissance architecture into the country. The town's Saint Multose' is an intact and living medieval church with later accretions, and the tholsel with its triple, eighteenth-century Dutch curvilinear gables – the last such to survive in the country – offer a more sophisticated visual environment than is to be found further west.

The combination of a safe harbour, the old-world atmosphere of a port town, the historic buildings and associations have given Kinsale an identity which fosters other things. The proliferation of small, smart restaurants in the narrow streets has given birth to a gourmet festival.

Some years ago I had an exhibition during this food festival. The festival was held in October, when tourism was at a low ebb, and its motive was to bring people into the town. The actuality went precisely as planned and the festival-goers revelled, dined and drank their way through the few days of the event. The usual complement of journalists from Irish, British and Continental papers was present to receive some of the perks of their trudging trade. As the days progressed the men and women of the media passed over into a state of hallucinatory good fellowship bordering on euphoria. It seemed certain that they would return to base and publish glowing accounts of Kinsale in their papers. One of the journalists covering culture did an interview with me about my exhibition. It promised to provide excellent publicity.

A year later I met the same journalist at a similar function and asked her what had happened to the interview. She looked embarrassed, sought escape, but then admitted that, well, yes, these did publish it, 'in a way'.

After my interviewer had returned from the gourmet festival she had written a wonderful profile of the artist. Unfortunately, her notes did not record the artist's name, nor could her memory be forced to divulge a clue to his identity. All had been obliterated by good fellowship. At length she got a name; it sounded right, so the article was published. The artist of vision whose name was used happened to be a serious abstractionist and he was not amused. The editor, too, was quite unreasonable, and dismissal was mentioned. However, one must take the long view of these things.

Contributor: Klaus Harvey moved to Kinsale in 2008 where he studied Permaculture and Practical Sustainability at Kinsale College of Further Education. He currently teaches Communications at the College, and has also been actively involved in Transition Town Kinsale, helping to promote a sustainable and resilient community.

He formed a band, The Good Rain, with whom he was the main singer and songwriter for nine years. He continues to perform in a solo capacity and runs open mic/tribute nights in the Tap Tavern in aid of Cork Simon Community. He is the author of college textbook 'Effective Communication'.

Reuben Harvey and the American Prisoners

During the American War of Independence in 1775, many American prisoners were held in Desmond Castle, also known as the French Prison, in Kinsale. The first batch to arrive comprised 33 rebels, who were housed there, and space and conditions were said to have been adequate for such purposes.

A Quaker merchant named Reuben Harvey was living in Cork city at the time, and as with many Cork Quakers, he had both commercial and personal links with both Quakers and other merchants in the American colonies. The Cork Society of Friends, being pacifists, set up a committee to raise funds for the relief of victims of the war.

Harvey was sympathetic to the American cause, and criticised the British government's actions. He was once brought before the mayor of Cork city to answer charges of assisting the American rebels, as he was said to have supplied them with British naval and military information. 'I would still adhere to their cause, believing it to be a just one, and them an oppressed people,' he wrote to the American Commissioners in Paris in 1783. He was also sympathetic to moves for Irish independence, so it is easy to see why he became unpopular with the British establishment.

However, he became better known for his interest in the worsening conditions of the prisoners in Desmond Castle. By 1781 it had become badly overcrowded, due to the increased number of American ships seized by the British Navy off the southwest coast of Ireland. It was reported that prisoners in Kinsale had minimal rations, and many were almost naked, sick or dying. In fact it was said that by 1782 sixty prisoners had already died there. Straw bedding was infested with vermin, and many died of smallpox. There were accusations of assault by prison guards on the captives, which included running their swords through the hammocks of sick prisoners. These accusations were written by an anonymous writer called 'Benevolous' in the *Hibernian Chronicle*, a Cork City journal. It is now understood that 'Benevolous' was Rev. William Hazlitt, a Unitarian minister living in Bandon, and father of William Hazlitt, the famous essayist.

The prison's agent, John How, wrote letters denying the accusations, and subsequently conditions improved slightly. Harvey also wrote letters of protest to the *Hibernian Chronicle*, and in 1782 he opened a subscription to aid the prisoners. With the help of these charitable donations, he delivered food, clothing, books and other necessities to the prisoners, and provided them with information about the current state of the war. Reuben Harvey often helped transport these items himself, travelling the fifteen miles from his Cork business to Kinsale, a route known for robbers.

Harvey and Hazlitt collaborated in their efforts to improve the conditions of the American prisoners by writing letters of protest to the British establishment. By the end of 1782, the war had ceased, and by the following spring the remaining prisoners had been released. Harvey continued to correspond with the American Commission in Paris, showing support for American independence and offering to serve the United States in the future. He also made several attempts to improve trade between America and Britain, despite the latter's trade restrictions.

Harvey's correspondence contains a number of letters to and from George Washington, including the following:

Headquarters, 23 June, 1783

Sir,

I was yesterday favoured with your letter of the 12th of February, and this day I transmitted the papers, which accompanied it, to the President of Congress, with a letter of which the enclosed is a copy.

Your early attachment to the cause of this country, and your exertions in relieving the distresses of such of our fellow citizens as were so unfortunate as to be prisoners in Ireland, claim the regard of every American, and will always entitle you to my particular esteem. I shall always be happy in rendering you every service in power, being with great truth, Sir,

Your very obedient servant,

GW

Headquarters 10th August 1783

Sir,

I am honoured with the Care of transmitting to you the enclosed Resolution of Congress, expressing the Sense which that August Body entertains of your Goodness to the American Prisoners in Ireland.

Impressed as I am with Sentiments of Gratitude to you, for this Expression of your Benevolence, I feel a very particular gratification on conveying to you the Thanks of the Sovereign Power of the United States of America, on an Occasion which, while it does honor to Humanity, stamps a Mark of particular Distinction on you. Wishing you the Enjoyment of Health, with every attendant Blessing, I beg you be persuaded that I am with very particular Respect & Regard sir,

   Your most Obedt Servt,

   GW

I learned of this piece of history when I moved to Kinsale in 2008. It is of particular interest to me because Reuben Harvey is my 7th great grandfather. John How, the prison agent to whom he protested about the conditions in the prison, is an ancestor of my sister-in-law, Jane Howe. She and my brother Patrick, have a son, my nephew, also named Reuben Harvey.

Contributor: Bernard McGouran

This story of my family is not unlike many others in that we have come about through Irish migration, which had world-wide changing effects as Ireland lost its sons and daughters for the greater good of all mankind.

The Road to Kinsale

Our father passed away during the hot summer of 1988 in Canada, he had just finished his Friday night dinner, BBQ Chicken Chalet. This was one of dad's favorite dinners, as the meat was charred and the skin very crispy. Our dad loved to eat tasty food, rich food, rib-stickler food and absolutely loved the black gravy with a generous amount of mashed potatoes. That would suit him fine along with bacon fried toast.

   Bernard "Red" McGouran was a sturdy big handsome fellow known for his ability to play hockey and baseball, as well as having a keen mind. He was our dad, our mother's husband and the father of 14 children who were raised as Irish Canadians.

The McGouran Brood

Dad died during that summer and Christmas was five months away. What was our mother going to do for the upcoming festive season as dad had always cooked the turkey dinner and Ma would be his kitchen helper? Christmas came, and it was horrible! There was no consoling Ma as the tears flowed while we were in the kitchen preparing the dinner. Glad that it finally came to an end, as all of us were teary-eyed as we attempted to eat our weepie dinner with some Christmas zeal.

We were all very thankful that our sister Kathleen and her husband Big Ron had invited the family to their country home in Lindsay, Ontario to celebrate the New Year. Travelling to Kath's and Ron's for a two day feast and sleep over was just what the family needed. Have a party and forget our feelings of utter despair and sadness towards our Ma's situation without her adored husband at her side.

The weather for New Years was cold and snowy, predictable for Canadian weather in late December-January. The whole family was nestled in at Kath's and Ron's resort home, looking out onto Sturgeon Lake. Food, food, food, beverages, card-playing tournaments, craic and boardgame playing, all this carrying on and it seemed too normal.

It did appear that our family had overcome the loss of our dad for the New Year's celebration. With all its revelry and the midnight countdown in play, we were back from the abyss of sorrow. We were the happy clan once again, looking forward to 1989 and what it might bring. Midnight struck and the kissing and joy-wishing started accompanied by Auld Lang Syne, it was great to be free of the weight of our dad's passing at that particular moment.

Not so fast, where is Ma?

Ma was in the kitchen at the table, sobbing by herself and she was inconsolable given the moment of reality that she was facing, no Bernard "Red" McGouran for her in 1989, or as long as she remained alive. Sitting down beside her I tried many, many times to get her to come round to acceptance of this void that would be present in her life. I told her that all her children and grandchildren would be the replenishment of her happiness. But it wasn't working, as Ma was still sobbing with pain and sorrow. I asked Ma if there was anything that would make her happy or bring her joy. Anything? Ma quickly responded, "Your dad was his happiest when he was home in Ireland"!

What came out of my mouth surprised even me, and still does somewhat, "Ma we are going to Ireland this coming spring".

While you the reader are not surprised, I will tell you that I had a conversation with my dad when he returned to Canada from a trip to Ireland in 1986 with my mother. The conversation consisted of my dad telling me to visit Ireland, our home, and that it could change my life for the good, and me saying to my dad that I would never set foot in Ireland. I had my selfish reasons back then and they served only me while ignoring my family's heritage.

There were eight of us that took the flight home to Ireland with our mother in May 1989, which included my wife Nancy. Ma was in her glory staying at Wynn's Hotel in Dublin, where she and dad had also stayed in previous years. The hotel personnel cheerfully remembered my dad and Ma from previous trips, or so they made out. We were a family again in happy mode, all things good and Irish, and Ma seemed to be delighted that she was home with a number of her children.

Growing up we were all schooled in Irelandisms from our dad's mother, Margaret (Maggie Ward) McGouran from Downpatrick, County Down, who ruled with an iron hand while she made sure that her other hand was filled with generosities for all deserving grandchildren. Ireland to us was what our grandmother (big Gran) told us or showed us as we were growing up. Ireland was our dad's people, we never gave much concern or to thought to our Ma's people because she married big Red McGouran.

Having dinner with our Ma in Dublin we asked about her father and where he was from in Ireland. We must have heard previously as children, but now had forgotten because being Irish was the Big Gran connection in our lives. Our mother came from less than meagre beginnings, and her life prior to being married to dad seemed unimportant or of little concern to us growing up as children. Her people were "poor" and Big Gran's people were doing okay. Ma's father was Charles Callaghan from a tiny place that we thought was called 'Tractor' in Cork. This assumption was predicated on an old birth certificate of Charles Callaghan, which was tattered and faded and only partially legible. We searched the map of Ireland and could not find such a place, and asked numerous times of people in Cork if they knew of or heard of such a place in Cork called Tractor. Cork is the largest County in Ireland and one cannot expect an average person to know of every small town or village. Sorry Ma, we can't find your dad's village/town because it's not on the map. We didn't find Tractor, Cork during our first visit.

That was May 1989. Nancy and I were determined to come back to Ireland the following year to find out what had become of my mother's family in Cork. We came back home to Ireland successive years, and didn't make any progress in finding Tractor, Cork until May 1992. The progress relates to a travel book that Nancy was reading which had a blurb on the General Registrar's Office on Liberty Street in Cork City. The comments in the book said that the employees at the Registrar's would take the time to search the old physical records for you. I wrote down my grandfather's name and year of birth, and village of Tractor, Cork on a blank piece of paper and handed it in at a window counter to an employee. After 10 or 15 minutes a clerk came back out from behind the counter and advised me that Tractor did not exist, but the village of Tracton did, and he had located a family of Callaghan's with Charles being one of them from the 1880's.

Over the moon! We have a winner! At least that's the way I felt hearing this great news about my Ma's dad. Soon I was in the possession of Charles Callaghan's birth certificate which listed his parent's information, as well as the district in which the Callaghan family lived during those times. All that information for 4 or 5 quid.

Charles Callaghan was born in the district of Ballyfeard in the Registrar's district of KINSALE. We had never imagined to look for Tractor near Kinsale, it would have helped to find Tracton.

Fast forward to May, 1993 as I drove with Nancy and my Ma to Kinsale, a town she had not seen or visited previously. Kinsale is picturesque and protected inland from the sea's bite with its narrow streets and tight lanes. It's a beautiful sight driving into Kinsale from the eastern approach and looks just like flowers sprouting from the garden, the pastel colors of the town's buildings appeared as if in a gigantic bowl of fruit straight ahead. In those days you could still smell the burnt peat in the air and feel the sea wind on your cheeks kissing you as you walked the narrow streets of Kinsale.

Ma was excited as a child on Christmas morning, but we still needed to find Tracton which by all accounts from the locals, only ten to 15 minutes away. I took a road out of town which slowly winded its way out of Kinsale, passed Nohoval and on to smaller secondary roads. Soon a sign post appeared on my right at a road junction which listed Tracton as the place we were now at: we had found Tracton, Charles Callaghan's birthplace.

Ma was filled with joy!

The Tracton Sign

I keep coming back to Tracton and Kinsale, it's where my family lives.

Post Script: Johanna O'Callaghan McGouran celebrated her 94th birthday in February 2018 and has 32 grandchildren, 25 great-grandchildren, and currently resides in a Senior's Retirement Home

Contributor: Dermot Ryan is a retired National School teacher and leads walks around the town as Kinsale Heritage Walks. He is also Secretary of the Kinsale Historical Society.

Kinsale, Our Heritage Town

Kinsale is best known for the Battle of 1601, which marked the end of Spanish domination of the New World, and the decline of the Gaelic way of life with the Flight of the Earls to Rome. Also of international importance was the sinking of the passenger liner the *Lusitania* off the Old Head of Kinsale in May 1915, a major factor in bringing the U.S. into World War One.

However, there is much more to this unique town, located in a safe harbour, in a strategic location on the trade route between Europe and North America. It was a base for earliest settlers, the Celts, and the Vikings, who called it the *Place of the Inner Fjord*, followed by the Normans and the English. Saint Multose (also known as Saint Eltin) established the first church and is reputed to have cursed the fortunes of the local residents, saying that only outsiders would prosper here. Another legend claims that *Carraig Oisín* at the World's End dates back to the Fianna, who watched for Roman invaders at the Old Head. Eight hundred years ago the Normans built Saint Multose Church, and the DeCourcey castles at the Old Head and Ringrone, and Kinsale became a walled town.

Their descendants developed Kinsale as a market town, building an important commercial and naval harbour which became a haven for local and visiting fishing fleets. Cromwell's forces destroyed the Carmelite Abbey in 1649, when many died, and women and children sent to work as slaves on the sugar plantations in the West Indies. Kinsale saw the landing of James II in his attempt to regain the English throne with the aid of Louis XIV and his flight to France after his defeat at the Battle of the Boyne by William of Orange in 1690. The Penal Laws are recalled by Mass Rocks and the street called Catholic Walk. The County Council office is located in a building that was the Workhouse during the Famine when relief schemes included building of the World's End Road to the west of town, and the area near the Tourist Office. As ships grew bigger the harbour declined and was partly filled in to create the centre of the town, which now depended on the military and fishing for survival. The Civil War of 1922 saw the destruction of Charles Fort, the Army and Police Barracks. The fishing and boat building industries declined so Kinsale became almost derelict, with many young people forced to emigrate.

Investment from Germany, France and, especially, the U.S. (Eli Lilly), helped economic recovery, and Kinsale became a tourist centre, famous for food, golf, angling and sailing as well as being acclaimed as a Heritage Town. The town has had a number of famous residents, Privy Councillor, Robert Southwell donor of the Gift (Alms) Houses; Alexander "Robinson Crusoe" Selkirk; The Irish Giant, Patrick Cotter O'Brien; writers Lennox Robinson and Robert Gibbings; Antarctic explorers, Mortimer and Timothy McCarthy who sailed with Scott and Shackleton.

Contributor: Fergal Browne (see above, Historical Kinsale)

Potato Riots in Kinsale – 21st November 1835

Ever since I first visited Kinsale Museum, many years ago, the 'Belgooly Proclamation' intrigued me. Dated 22nd November 1835 and in a small black frame hanging in the old Court Room, the word 'Belgooly' is the largest word on the whole proclamation.

In 1835, Thomas Jennings, a prominent Cork Businessman, owned a starch mill in Belgooly. This stood behind the current ruins of the flour mill, which later became part of Belgooly Distillery.

The proclamation threatens the penalty of transportation for anybody found taking part in a march to Belgooly with the intention of pulling down Jennings' starch mill. It states that the magistrates of Kinsale received information on oath concerning this march and threatens anyone caught taking part in it with transportation for seven years. George A. Daunt of Newborough signed this proclamation along with Edward J. Heard (Sovereign of Kinsale), John J. Heard, John Thomas Cramer of Rathmore House, Kinsale, John Cuthbert, Thomas Knolles of Oatlands and William Newman.

Anybody looking at the Proclamation would wonder why Kinsale townspeople would be so incensed that they would look to march to Belgooly to destroy the mill. Now, a recently discovered letter written to the Cork Evening Standard on 21st November 1835 gives a detailed background to what was going on.

Proclamation displayed in Kinsale Museum, dated 1835

Like many letters written to newspapers at that time, the letter is anonymous. The author signs themselves 'A Friend to Peace', however, it is clear which side he supports.

He begins the letter with a flourish: 'The Uprising has commenced' and later in the letter bemoans the fact that there are only a few police and about 150 troops available in Charles Fort, 'all together inadequate to preserve the peace'. He then goes on to describe what had occurred in the town of Kinsale earlier that day, the 21st November 1835.

It appears that Thomas Jennings had earlier that year begun buying up potatoes in the area for use in the mill to manufacture starch. This, naturally, caused the price of potatoes to increase rapidly. Furthermore, Jennings also purchased the poor quality vegetables which would normally have been ignored by food retailers and instead would have been affordable by the poor. After all, potatoes both good and bad were literally 'grist to the mill'.

Being priced out of the market for their primary commodity brought immediate hardship on the poor of Kinsale and the surrounding area. In protest, and as described by the anonymous letter writer, a large crowd gathered at Worlds End and Scilly, 'armed with swords, boarding pikes, saws, sticks and whatever could be calculated for offence', and marched with flags through the town as far as the market place. They shouted their intention to march to Belgooly to pull down the starch mill.

Here the letter writer becomes somewhat disingenuous, stating that they threatened destruction to 'a poor miller'. However, Thomas Jennings was one of the largest manufacturers in Cork, owning a number of soda water distillation premises. His descendants would later build Brookfield House, on the outskirts of Cork City, which in the early 2000's became part of University College Cork. He was anything but poor.

The letter proceeds to inform us that, while the crowd had assembled in Market Square, one of the county magistrates approached them and recommended that they disperse and return quietly to their homes. As he did so, one of the leaders of the march stood behind him, brandishing a sword over his head. The crowd showed no sign of dispersing until they were addressed by the local priest. According to the letter writer the priest 'spoke a few words and immediately the storm was immediately appeased – the mob dispersed and in ten minutes all was as tranquil as before'. 'What a blessing it would be', continued the letter writer, 'if this formidable power was always wielded thus to promote peace!'.

The author of the letter was even more concerned at the thought that the 'illegal assembly', as he describes it, had been called together by 'public proclamation'. He describes how written placards had been posted around the town on the previous Sunday calling on the tradesmen 'and all others interested in cheap food' to meet as soon as possible to 'pull down the offensive mill and inflict condign punishment on the daring miller'. He notes that the arms carried by the crowd fall well within the criteria covered by the laws designed to repress 'tumultuous assemblies'. He concludes the letter by stating that the magistrates of the town had at that time assembled.

Belgooly Mills, drawn in 1857

The proclamation which now hangs in Kinsale Museum was clearly the result of the magistrates deliberations. Its threat of deportation, coupled with the warning from the priest, clearly had an effect on the crowd, as the starch mill at Belgooly was still in place in 1837 when Samuel Lewis compiled his 'Topographical Dictionary of Ireland'.

The attitude of the letter-writer shows a devotion to free-market economics, with an unfettered market dictating the price of a commodity, irrespective of the hardship that causes, would be mirrored a few years later by Charles Edward Trevelyan, Assistant Secretary to the British Treasury during the Great Famine. Throughout the Famine years, Trevelyan was anxious to make sure that excessively cheap food would not be provided to the starving masses, for fear of the adverse impact it would have on the market – and on the landowners and millers who profited from the sale.

The proclamation in Kinsale Museum is an interesting relic of a tumultuous period in Kinsale History – a foreshadow of the dark spectre of famine which hung over the town, and the country, at the time.

Kinsale Memories

Contributor: Cristina Galvin lived in Kinsale until the age of eleven before moving with her family to Co. Galway. Her writing has been published in the Irish Times, Noir by Noir West *(a collection of dark fiction from the west of Ireland) and she won the Powers Short Story Award. After several years working in public health research in Russia and U.S., she returned to Galway where she did an M.A. in writing. She is now based in Wales, where she works as a psychotherapist.*

Revisiting

I grew up on Main Street. A terraced house on a narrow lane that only in aspirational Kinsale could be classified as 'Main'. In a ramshackle house built for children and elf-sized people, my parents opened a restaurant they called The Vintage. I remember 'Strawbs', the gentle, red-nosed giant who delivered berries every Tuesday in summer, ducking in the front-door to avoid adding another gash to the map of scabby bumps on his baldy head. Our house was old. Legend had it that the eight spooky timber beams that spanned the low-ceilinged dining room and were festooned with a slew of plastic grape-vines to intensify the cellar-like feel, hailed from the hull of a 400-year old ship.

Many nights as a child I sat on the stairs knees-to-chest in pink nightie, observing the bustle below. Air filled with hum on customers' arrival. Staccato shouts from the kitchen— *Horgans Seated! Table 3 Away!*—intermingled with the rising fever of Mozart's clarinet quintet, sounds of chinking glasses, bursts of laughter.

Waitresses scurried back and forth, shepherding platters of delectable dishes to hungry guests—black sole with sea spinach and saffron aioli, pear and pumpkin soup, desserts of tipsy pudding in mulled wine. Dicky-bowed barmen weaved their way through dinner-plated traffic, wine-glasses held high on trays above their heads. Steam and hot-pan spatter billowed from the kitchen. Whiffs of charred meat and onion that seared the night like a butcher's blade. And me on the stairs surveying the scene, simultaneously feeling part and apart from it all, sudden tears twanging my eyes.

Tucked up in a creaky cot at night in the top-floor skylight room and hedged in by an army of teddies to dupe any kidnappers as to the presence of child-in-bed, I would say my prayers in the company of winking stars and watch car-lights scud across the ceiling. On nights when stars refused to peep, the hammer of rain on the window would lull me to disjointed dreams and I'd wake to early morning sounds of mewling gulls and clang of ropes on boats down at the marina, an auditory bicker and jangle that still reverberates in my blood despite now living inland and elsewhere.

Sundays the restaurant was closed. Mum brought us to Mass. Dad stayed home 'cos he was angry at God. You could buy squillions of penny sweets with your 10p Sunday pocket money back then, especially next door at Nora's. Nora was the apple-cheeked sweetshop lady who, with smile as bright as her neon green cardigan and using her shovel-like hands as a cola-bottle scooper, would give us double servings alongside the sherbet and lucky bags we bought in her shop.

Some Sundays, if we were good, we'd get to go with my mum and dad to Skippers Bistro for Sunday lunch. Dad loved Sunday lunch 'cos it meant he didn't have to cook. I did too 'cos it meant I got to see him.

The street above our pokey back-garden, accessed through a steep forest of nettles and cuggles, had the best view in Ireland. No surprise then that my flying dreams started here. Oh, the joyous feeling of spreading my wings wide, running down Higher Street, taking off on the slant and swooping down over the chimneypots. First a flit to sniff wild roses in Hurleys' brambled jungle, then to Cronins' DIY store with the grunting floorboards and shelves piled with Everything-Both-Needful-and-Not. A furtive glance in Boland's' window opposite, Kinsale's sole posh shop. Can a six-year-old feel lust? Boland's' aisles of tantalising toys, chocolate bars in shiny wrapping and promise of blue-ice Slush-Puppies certainly incited it.

Nearly forty years on and the nagging pull has never left.

So, here I am—stranger back on fly-in visit to her old home-town.

Wings and body remembering the drill, soften into the muscle of the wind. Up, up and away, bee-lining for the harbour. Wheeling across the water to Castlepark, my chest fills with briny breath. Belly-brimming the waves like a swallow, I round the bluff to the secret cove where my friends and I discovered new worlds in rockpools with each tide's turning.

A trouncing wave hurls me to James' Fort. I bounce gratefully on grass by a blackberry ditch. Tart berry-tangs un-dizzy me, yet the memory of dad's lush monkfish—an atoll of pillowy white afloat in glossy ink from the blackberries we collected here—somehow undoes me. Recalling the relentless drizzle that drenched us on our foraging, our moaning to go home and the buckets of wormy sludge that got sifted later to make mouth-watering sauce for refined diners, lifts me up again with a laugh. And, so it is I'm soaring on the breeze to Summercove.

After heady sips of sunset with local blow-ins at the Bulman, it's on to Charles Fort. No wish to hover here. From these battlements the White Lady leapt and still she ghosts.

What made her pitch herself to roiling waves? I've always wondered. Perhaps the incantatory pull of the sea. I understand this bewitchment.

For if you live by the sea, swim in the sea, learn to read its sounds, smells, tastes, tides, submergent moods, it will percolate your days, your dreams, your bones so the need to dunk in the sea becomes greater almost than your need for air.

Having dunked, you must just remember to come up again.

Coasting townwards, silver light and shadow play piano on the water, beckoning me in. Down I dive and further down, to where freedom's coldest. Then bolt the surface with lung-busting whoop. Back on Kinsale pier, I'm spent. Shaking water from my wing-feathers, limbs tingle gratitude, my lips purplish-blue.

In childhood dreams, waning wing-power always spelled the ending. Flapping hard to stay aloft proved fruitless, being forced to land and worse, awaken.

Homesick for a place that exists no longer, I've returned to where I first took flight. On this street with the view overlooking the town, I stand feet firm, grounded. Backway's gone, no pokey garden—all dwellings built for elf-sized folk long since expanded. Gourmet kitchens, genteel shops abound, while new faces replace all us who scarpered. How strange to see some smiles embody souls I recognise (one of whom feels quite like me).

Last slats of light ignite the hills. Shadows sidle up the headlands to the forts standing sentry on the bay. Seagulls jabber. Breeze and boats make jazzy clang. Tide's rolling in.

What gift to revisit.

Contributor: Sheila Forde

My late father-in-law was born in Kinsale. His parents were born and raised there too. He always had a desire to re-connect with his home, and for that reason he bought a cottage in Sandycove. So the family has owned a holiday home in Sandycove for the last 45 years. That is why I have spent many summers and school breaks over the last thirty years at our little cottage overlooking the sea.

From Sandycove to Kinsale – A Memoir

My father-in-law bought a holiday home in Sandycove over 45 years ago as he wanted his "own wall" to look over, out to sea, fulfilling his long-held desire to re-connect with Kinsale, his birth place. Many years went by, with the family commuting between Dublin and Kinsale for week-ends. That gave my husband great childhood memories of the town, and nearby Sandycove. The tradition of spending week-ends and summers in Sandycove has continued into the next generation, enriching our children with the same special memories of this beautiful part of Cork.

The senses have a heightened awareness once the car comes down the hill from the Cork road, with the apprehension that special memories and sights may have vanished. But on seeing the 'Welcome to Kinsale' sign on the boat with exuberant flowers, a warm feeling of home spreads through my bones. My first mission is a walk around the town in pursuit of my old haunts, the pubs, the quirky shops I always visit, and my favourite gourmet restaurants. Once this routine is complete, we cross Kinsale bridge and follow the narrow winding road to Sandycove.

Turning the final corner to the cottage, the island comes into view, and the ritual of counting the goats begins. When we first visited Sandycove there were 25-30 of them. For the last two years the goat count is a total of five. I can only assume that they are all the one sex. According to the locals, a farmer brought a few goats over to the island on his boat in the 1960s, when farming trends changed, and the humble goat became less popular. Up to then, the island had been uninhabited, with no animal life. The logic was that the goats would keep the grass down. For many years a few goats were added annually to the flock to lower the risk of in-breeding. Eventually, the goats were forgotten about, and with no new partners being brought to the island.

I assume that inbreeding resulted, reducing the longevity and resilience of the animals. This is perhaps one reason for the decline in population today, along with the increasingly severity of winters.

In the Sandycove cottage, seagulls squawking and the sound of waves crashing on the rocks fill my ears, serenading me to sleep at night. Then I am awakened with the sunrise over the island, and a misty shimmer of rising goats, eager to suck the early morning dew from the grass, since there is no fresh water on the island. Peering over "my wall" I watch the cormorants swoop and gracefully dive into the water in pursuit of their prey. The 'Billy Divers', my husband called them as a child, and the name has carried on into the present generation. I follow the tide times to enhance my chances of catching a glimpse of the 'Sandycove Seal' who swims in and out on the turn of the tide in pursuit of mackerel. Many hours are spent watching him raising his head above the water, diving, disappearing, and sometimes being lucky enough to see him re-appearing much further down the creek. 'The Sandycove Seal' still performs his daily routine and follows our little rubber dinghy out in the cove. It is highly unlikely he is the same one over all these years but the same tradition has carried on from one generation of the family to the next.

An elderly local man was a great story teller, a believer in *'piseogs'*, who narrated many stories of the sea in the area. One Easter he shared a belief that pods of dolphins visiting the cove signalled a very good summer approaching. How right was the man whose soul was immersed in the seas and skies of Sandycove. A month later a pod of twelve dolphins introducing the hot summer of 2006 made a grand entrance into Sandycove in acrobatic dance, displaying their talent of jumping in duos, synchronized waltzing in the waters, while exhaling great puffs of air and water sprays.

This same man knew every nook and cranny of the natural surroundings. Once he led me down steps to the rocks at 'Rock House', pulling back briars and overgrowth on the wall, unveiling the engraved names of several men who had died at sea in the area in past times. This led me to believe there are many secrets these waters and rocks may silently hold forever. The house itself was a granary in pre-famine times and a grain storage facility in the 1840s. The idyllic setting was also used by smugglers in days gone by for landing illicit cargoes.

Kinsale and Sandycove will never cease to entertain you, with the constant mingling of visitors, immigrants, adventurers, creative artists and most of all the locals. The area offers an abundance of hospitality, laughter, and a unique appreciation and pride in the sea and the town. There is a glint in the eyes of the locals on a clear bright day, all drawn together to glory in the water's offerings. A social chatter begins as people battle their way into wetsuits. Kayaks, body boards, wake boards bring added colour to the scene. A view presented to me of Sandycove re-inventing dancing at the crossroads.

Dreaming, reminiscing on the magic of the sea, gazing at children holding fishing rods in search of sprat, reminding me of the time I searched the towns of coastal Cork in pursuit of a prawn pot as a gift to our sons. The pot was purchased and set overnight. The boys eagerly retrieved it next day towing it behind the dinghy to discover it was full of baby crabs and not a prawn in sight. I lean across 'my wall' smiling, remembering the crab race as all were released back to the sea at the Sandycove slipway.

Contributor: My name is Robin Renwick. I lived in Kinsale from the age of 9 (1990), living first in Summer Cove and then moving into the town centre, living in various houses. I spent most of my time in Kinsale, living with my mother and sister in Green Hill House, which the poem is about. It is the house on the steps up to the Bowling Green.

I lived there until it was sold in 2011, nearly twenty years, I would imagine, if not more. We sold the house and my mother moved to Clonakilty. It has since been completely renovated. I have enclosed a picture of when it was sold. Quite different to how it is now. When we sold it, it was literally starting to fall down, hence the safety railings you see in the picture.

Green Hill

Old worn perch atop green hill house
my youth, a haze; passed by in misspent truth.
Many will know the steps and rails
the wettened wall and moss covered flow;
the age old sea bleached stone.
Those steps serve path for bowling green and compass hill,
To Friday's Justice served all sworn.
From Old State's hand; a view from but a sill.
Parking fines, planning requests, and misdirected youths
passed by my perch as life and wisdom followed suit.
Stolen kisses, midnight elopes, and devilish grins
told tales that rampant youth does bring.

I watched walkers, sailors, artists and drunks
scale steps to the municipal hall.
Watched gleeful tourists curiously saunter
wishing history to tell its honest all.
But if green hill house would whisper then,
the magic would all be lost.
Just like the day the old dispensary died, made anew;
all forgotten like the moss.

Contributor: George Harding's family has a close connection to Ballymacus, and two of his three children were born while he and Nuala lived there in the 1980s. George (also known as Daw) ran the family business, Harding Cycles in Cork, and took early retirement to study archaeology at University College, Cork. He has published two collections of poetry, My Stolen City and Last Bus to Pewterhole Cross, and his work was included in a Junior Cert textbook. He and Nuala currently divide their time between their home in Cork City and Ballymacus.

Coming to Kinsale

It was the early 1950s. George Harding sailed through Pewterhole Cross on his bicycle, followed closely by his wife, Kay on her 'Silver Swallow' bicycle (as she called it). They flew down the hill into Kinsale town, where they parked their bikes outside a little café, had some tea and relaxed for a brief spell. Restarting the journey through Summer Cove, they sped past ancient Charles Fort, uphill and yonder until they reached the cul-de-sac sign that was their marker for their destination; Ernest Walker had told them to go through the gates at Daly's' cottage and that his house was a short distance down the hill.

They were lucky: the sky was blue, the sea was blue and the corn danced along the headland towards the Sovereign Islands. They immediately knew they had landed in a magical place, in a landscape that far outstripped any they had encountered in their weekend trips throughout the counties of Cork, Kerry and Tipperary. Ernest was happy to meet them, and they were soon sipping tea and eating freshly baked scones from May's oven. Ernie was a farmer, and he had told George that there were a couple of vacant old cottages on his land that could be used for holidays for anybody interested in getting away from the city for a while. The cottages, once occupied by farm labourers, had become unused due to the advent of the tractor and modern machinery. Now, they were ready to let out as holiday homes to anyone adventurous enough to take the opportunity. Initially there was no electricity or gas, and water was available internally from a gravity flow which occasionally reduced to a trickle if there happened to be a long dry spell of weather. For many, there would have been more reasons to leave than to stay.

Despite all these drawbacks, luckily George and Kay decided there and then to bite the bullet and agree terms to take one of the cottages for the coming summer. These pioneers had been used to staying in *An Óige* hostels throughout Munster in somewhat primitive conditions, cooking meals on Primus stoves and sleeping on bunk beds. To them, the thought of spending a summer in similar circumstances was not off-putting.

Thank God and his blessed Mother for that – as my own mother used to exclaim after hearing good news about something or other. For me, it was the best decision that they ever made in their lives.

Ernest Walker and George Harding came together through the sport of cycling. Ernest fancied himself as a racing cyclist and used to frequent the cycle races held in Cork in the 1940s, which normally took place on Sundays. George happened to be one of the officials who organised them and, as so often happens, fate intervened.

Ernie was a Protestant and could not partake in sporting events that were held on Sundays. So he approached George to explain his dilemma: as the results of each race would appear in the *Cork Examiner* the following week, Ernie would be in trouble if he'd been lucky enough to procure a place on the winning rostrum. If his name were to appear on the sports pages, his sporting career would in all probability be terminated. George understood the situation well, as his own mother was a Protestant, and he assured Ernie that he need not worry. George came up with a simple answer: he would enter a fictitious name for the farmer from Kinsale. Ernie did in fact gain second or third place on occasion – and the people back in his home town were none the wiser.

A lifelong relationship blossomed between the two men's families, remaining long after the Walkers sold their farm in the mid 1970s. Ernie and May had no children, and after a couple of hundred years at the heart of a working farm, the old farmhouse in which they lived began to crumble. Once synonymous with this corner of Kinsale, the Walker name faded with it into history. All of a sudden it was the 20th century and Ireland had just entered the Common Market – later the European Union – and farming began to enter a new era.

Last Bus to Pewterhole Cross

Half past midnight the bus pulled in
he alighted and heaved the army rucksack
sardined with victuals to his shoulders
and strode into the moon filled night.
High above somewhere Telstar was nearer
the stars that sent their music to him.
Silent as a ghost he passed the graveyard
And paused at Barniarrig to savour the lights
at the top of the sea.
On up past Garraha and Bawnavota
bats winging drunkenly like leaves
in a winter gale. Along here bent trees
in the ditches silhouetted like mourners
at a giant's funeral. Tired now
he ambled past Rathmore's high wood

sighed as the road sloped downwards
and spied the first glints of the gas light
winking and flickering from our window.
They let me stay up that night
to enable me to spot the spying Russians
and welcome the traveller from the east.
"There's a sweet for you in there"
he said as he flopped in his chair
and exclaimed "what a beautiful night!"
He invited me to unlace his big boots
tied up beyond his ankles.
Years later I overheard
"He'll never stand in his father's shoes"
but that night I grew a little
when I broadened my skinny shoulders
and pulled those boots from his tired feet.

Contributor: Augustus Young, Cork-born poet and writer has vivid memories of family holidays in Ballymacus. His highly acclaimed first volume of memoirs, Light Years *was recently joined by a second,* Heavy Years (Quartet, 2014), *based on his professional career as James Hogan, an epidemiologist. This extract is from a new, as yet unpublished memoir,* Family Legends.

A 'Capable Girl' from Kinsale

My mother had a way with fires. In five minutes she could have the hearth in the front-room ablaze with blocks of wood, and the chimney too. That called for salt and a newspaper screen to prevent smoking the house. Afterwards she threw on slack, wet crushed coal. While the chimney was on fire we went out into the garden to watch the sparks fly. Sometimes there were flames like from the Dunlop's chimney on the way into town. Once, on a picnic, she set fire to a hillside in Roberts Cove with a primus stove and appeased the enraged farmer by helping to put it out. We watched from a safe distance.

    My mother dealt with people on my father's behalf. On holiday in Ballymacus something happened with Jackie Ryan which annoyed him. I think she did not respond to his hallo, or maybe it was about hogging the communal boat. When my mother had a word with Mrs Ryan, she responded with the immortal line, 'Professor Hogan does not enter into my scheme of things'. Bad feeling lingered, and within the family too, as my mother blamed my father for making her fall out with a neighbour.

    Her people had been living in the Kinsale area near Nohoval for four generations and felt outsiders as they didn't own land. The O'Neills were artisans. In the early 19th century a tanner migrated from the northwest of Spain to work in a Huguenot leather factory, married a local girl, and took her name. My mother's father was a roof-thatcher by trade. But when slating came in, he rented a farmyard to breed turkeys. He died in his forties of heart disease, leaving eight children. The only childhood memory my mother divulged was of coaxing the birds down from the trees with a bean-pole.

While growing up we did not speak of her family. She married without their consent, as my father did not come with land. The only sign that she was in contact with her mother was a live turkey arriving at Christmas. Her family was an absence that was mythologized by hearsay, and chance encounters with people who knew them. Not least Bob O'Donoghue [aka the poet Robert O'Donoghue] of the Cork Examiner, who claimed that the famous romance between the bachelor professor and an eighteen-year old girl ended the Great Depression. On holidays, driving from Minane Bridge to Summer Cove, her silence passing through Nohoval was respected as mourning for her mother, whose funeral she wasn't allowed to attend.

In the late fifties, Ballymacus was a veritable Hollywood. Jackie Ryan was a child star in *The Adventures* of *Jacqueline*. Then there was the Murphy family. One daughter, Moonyeen, had been Virginia Mayo's secretary. The other, Fidelma, left the Abbey Theatre training school to star in Pat Boone's film "Never Put it in Writing" (1964).

The eldest son had been Bulganin and Malenkov's Russian interpreter on their visit to London. I was half in love with Fidelma but was hopelessly superior when talking to her, not unlike Tony Curtis in *Some Like It Hot* (1959). Two years later my father was dead. And yet I recall how godlike he looked breasting the waves making sure his mane of hair did not get wet. There was ancient oak wood on one side of the creek, and a heather and furze hill in purple and yellow flower on the other. Pheasant would rise up from it unexpectedly.

Bob remarked on my mother's resemblance to Charlie Chaplin's young wife, Oona, the daughter of Eugene O'Neill, the playwright: dark, lightly-built beauties with olive skin and crinkly Spanish hair.

The Chaplins holidayed near Kinsale, he said Bob liked to think these two 'capable girls' with complicated, older husbands were half-sisters, though, in the words of Ronald Reagan, 'the facts and the evidence tell me otherwise'. The Chaplins were better known to stay in Waterville.

My mother was a doer. When anything electrical had to be fixed she did it herself. I remember the fear of seeing her hanging from the ceiling, changing a light bulb. One dreadful night she fell downstairs over the top landing. She used to climb on the stove to put clothes on the kitchen washing line. It gave rise to an infant chorus, 'Mammy on the stove!' (sung to the tune of 'Brennan on the Moor'). She, though, was not above histrionics when reproved by my father when I broke a violin bow. It rebounded on him, but not me.

Our father in his sad gentle way explained, more as a fact than a judgement, 'Your mother is a wicked woman', and she could be. Nobody enjoyed more telling bitterly funny stories about the folly of others. In my middle years, I came to appreciate that letting off homeopathic doses of malice was the antidote to her unfailing courtesy outside the family. It made her such a pleasure to meet that people would tell her things they shouldn't.

She drove and cooked merely out of necessity. Returning from the country after buying apples for the winter from a farm, she swung in the gate and took a short-cut across the lawn, skidding. Next day mushrooms sprouted on the skid-marks. We had omelettes for dinner. And once driving down the steep hill at the far side of Kinsale the brakes snapped, and she negotiated the descent by handbrake, using reverse when it got out of control. My mother was a disaster waiting to happen so she could show to advantage.

My mother was not naive, or a prude. As grandchildren began to live their lives differently from what we were brought up to, she was more accepting than our generation.

In later years, her dramatic sense expressed itself in the timing of surprise visits. Once in the early hours of the morning, her knock on our door in my Belsize Park Gardens flat in London was a theatrical coup. On impulse she had taken Slattery's bus and the ferry from Cork. We went to Brian Friel's, 'Philadelphia Here I Come' in the West End and after the interval sat out the remaining acts in the lobby, talking. My mother said 'it was better than a play', and it was (the Friel was at the end of a long run). In many ways her life was a play within a play and we children were her best audience.

Contributor: Donal Herlihy, formerly of The Harp & Shamrock in The Glen, now the café, OHK [Audio recording by Ruth McDonnell]

Our home was a fine three storey house in a part of Kinsale known as the Glen. The house doubled as a licensed premises with the grand patriotic name of The Harp and Shamrock. It had been in the family for generations, and was a home ideally suited to the dreams and imagination of a young boy. It served me well for twenty happy years.

The bar was very straightforward, no frills, no nonsense type, with a huge solid mahogany front door to the street on one side, and the bar on the other. None of your weather doors, porches or swing doors to keep the weather out and the heat in. When that door was thrown open by my mother in the depths of winter at half past ten on a frosty morning, the temperature in the bar quickly adjusted itself to that of the sub-zero one in the street. Yet, it rarely seemed to bother the local customers standing at the bar. Their heated discussions on hurling, football, fishing and world affairs warmed the atmosphere like a modern day heating system.

The item which always focused best in my memory of the kitchen was the large picture of the Cunard liner S.S. Mauretania which hung above the meals table . Measuring about four foot by three, in beautiful colour, it showed the ship cutting through the bright blue ocean with the sea creaming at her bow and her four red funnels billowing smoke. Across the bottom of the picture were the words 'S.S. Mauretania fastest liner in the world , across the Atlantic in less than four and half days'. That picture dominated the kitchen and primed my imagination almost daily for all of eighteen years. Hardly a day passed when either at breakfast, dinner or tea and oft times all three., I would mentally leave the kitchen and find myself standing on the bridge of the Mauretania, binoculars around my neck and with a gale force wind blowing on my face: we were steaming for America.

Years later as a young Radio Officer in the Merchant Navy I did numerous crossings of that same North Atlantic Ocean in storm force weather and with the ship rolling on her beam ends I would mentally return to that nice warm kitchen in the Glen and gladly watch the S.S. Mauretania crossing the Atlantic in less than four and half days.

Contributor: William Hall, the grand-nephew of Major Richard Meade of Ballymartle House, spent many of his childhood summers living with his grandmother, Dorothea Fowle (nee Meade) in Summercove during the 1930's. His parents were married in St. Catherine's Church, Ringcurran in April 1922. His mother, Dorothea Hall, was Kinsale's first practicing Physiotherapist, working with wounded soldiers from the Great War. William has a keen interest in the history of his family and their connections to Kinsale. He now lives in England.

Growing up in Summer Cove in the 1930s

I spent most of my early years at Summer Cove with my grandmother because much of the time my parents were in India. The village was unusual in a way because of the number of relicts from the days of British rule who still resided there due, perhaps, to its proximity to Charles Fort, which had been the British garrison. Almost without exception they were unmarried daughters or widows of the former British regime. As the days about which I'm writing are long gone, and there are not many left to remember them I thought that a few notes on what I recall might be of interest.

My early schooling was at a very small school in Summer Cove run by Miss Willis. We had copybooks with the letters of the alphabet printed in a line which we had to copy between lines meticulously, and it is a pity that they don't have them nowadays. Other pupils whom I recall were Ivan and Norman Woodrow of the Manse, Winifred Perry from Lower Road, Neal Pierce from Rathmore House, and Robin Allport. The little school was a survival from the days of the British garrison when it had been full of the children of British troops' families. Exercise books were only for homework - all work at school was written on slates with slate pencils obtainable from the village shop.

St. Catherine's church at the top of the hill in the parish of Rincurran, to which my grandmother went twice every Sunday with me in tow, was Protestant, though the majority of the village were Roman Catholic. On Sundays the Roman Catholics came in from outlying farms and villages through Summer Cove on their way to Mass in Kinsale. There were several services to allow for those who had to come a long distance, and in the evening the sound of the Angelus bell would drift across the harbour to Summer Cove. Some of the farmers went to church on their flat farm carts with the farmer holding the reins and sitting on the shafts to stop them lifting when going up the hill with the family sitting on the cart. The iron-hooped wheels on the stony road made a terrific clatter.

A number of the women in Kinsale used to wear the traditional west Cork black hooded cloak and on Sunday afternoons the students from the large seminary in Kinsale would come through Summer Cove on their weekly walk and go on to Charles Fort. We always knew the beach on the seaward side of Charles Fort as the Sally Port. but I see on maps that the Sally Port was situated at Middle Cove, although no-one corrected us. A footpath led from Charles Fort to Middle Cove and Lower Cove and thence out to Preghane Point, where one could watch the huge rollers coming in from the Atlantic in a storm and crashing against the rocks with the spray being blown right over the top of the cliff. If I recall correctly there was only one house at both Middle Cove and Lower Cove.

Summer Cove had a post office-cum-shop across the road from Duncarrig run by Mrs. Kavanagh, a pub run by Mr. Barry (now the Bulman) and a small grocers shop run by Mr. Barry's sister. Sweets were five for one halfpenny (pronounced 'haypenny'), bottles of fizzy lemonade were tuppence (two pence) - old pennies of course. We used to get milk and cream from O'Leary's farm in the village. The post office had a public telephone but as it was mounted on the wall of the shop one's conversations were listened to by anyone who happened to be there. There had been a previous post office run by the Coleman family lower down the village near the quay. I was told that the telephone was not there for the convenience of the residents of Summer Cove, but because it was the only communication for the Coastguard if there were an emergency. Sometime in the 1930s there had in fact been an emergency when a small coaster trying to get into the harbour to escape a furious gale had been driven onto the rocks below Charles Fort, and the crew rescued by breeches-buoy.

Miss Barry's shop was just across the road from the slipway and one night in a very severe storm a piece of flotsam, thrown into the air when a wave hit the slip, was caught by the wind and hurled through an upstairs window. On the quayside there were a few old howitzer cannon barrels. I have no idea why they were there or how they got there – perhaps the army were trying to move them from Charles Fort and found them too heavy to drag up the hill to Kinsale.

Amongst other things, the shop sold the slate pencils, and pens with steel nibs for school and small bottles of ink with cork stoppers. 'J' nibs were preferred as they were less scratchy to write with. Talking of slate, there was a plentiful supply of roofing slates at Charles Fort because inside the fort the British had built modern barracks with slate roofs, but when the barracks were burnt down in the "Troubles" in 1922 (after the British had gone) the slates in their thousands were left lying on the ground. They could be collected in a wheelbarrow and were very useful for edging paths in gardens. No one in Summer Cove, or Kinsale for that matter, ever had to go short of the best quality Welsh slates for repairing roofs.

Anyone could walk into Charles Fort and go into the deep dark dungeons which had been built three hundred years earlier. A few of the iron rings to which prisoners used to be shackled were still on the walls, and one of the dungeons was built over a cleft in the rocks below, through which waves used to force up air with a very ghostly moaning sound. My grandmother's eldest son wrote an article about the legend of the ghost of the White Lady which was published in the Wide World magazine.

No-one in the village owned a car (or a telephone), but as taxis were 2/6d (over £3 in today's money) for the mile to Kinsale, most people walked, and carried their shopping back. One could also hire an "inside car" which, to my young mind, was a rather frightening horse-drawn conveyance. It was a black box on two wheels with a little metal step at the back to enable one to climb in. As we were already on a hill, the weight of passengers entering it used to tip up the shafts so high that the horse was almost lifted off the ground. When the door was shut it was nearly pitch dark inside as there was only one very small window a few inches wide which was too high for me up to look out of. The horse had to make a real effort to pull this vehicle up the hill and it was with great difficulty that we restrained ourselves from slipping off the seat. Sometimes Willie and Vida Nash from Knockrobin would send their pony and trap to take us over for tea.

My grandmother's house was a three storied terraced house half way down the hill looking over the harbour, with a large garden. As the house faced south west it caught the full force of the gales blowing in from the Atlantic, and I can still recall the furious drumming of the rain on the windows in a storm, as if someone were hurling gravel at them. The upstairs windows which were more exposed had wooden shutters. Inside the front door there was a second door which, in a gale, had to be closed before the front door could be opened to prevent the gale rushing through the house and sweeping everything off the hall table. The house was rented at £30 per annum from a Miss Daunt. but prior to the Daunts it had been owned by the Heard family, and the name Heard had been scratched on one of the window panes.

As there was no electricity in the village cooking was by Primus stove and steamer in the summer, and coal range in the winter. Toast was made on a "toaster" which was a flat square of metal with a wire mesh on which to put the bread to be placed on top of the Primus. To save matches, we used to tear newspaper pages into wide strips and fold them over to make spills which were lit from the drawing room fire for lighting the Aladdin and other oil lamps and candles. To supplement my pocket money I used to earn 1d for every dozen spills which I made. The paraffin was brought originally in a tank loaded on to a horse drawn cart but latterly a small lorry was used. The Shannon Electric Scheme offered electricity at 8d. per unit but at that price there were no takers. The equivalent today would be about £1.28 in our money!

My grandmother employed Mr. Carberry once a week to work in her garden which consisted of a flower garden, vegetable garden and orchard. There was no need to use manure as there was an everlasting supply of seaweed on the shore by the slipway. It was brought up in a wheelbarrow and trundled through the hall to the backdoor as there was no other way into the garden. Although the house was on the cliff above the sea, in the winter storms the salt spray would be carried by the wind right over the house into the garden, which didn't do the plants any good.

I have now seen Kinsale transformed beyond all possible expectations and although it is marvellous to see all the prosperity which has flooded in, I still have some nostalgia for the quiet life which I was fortunate enough to experience in comfort in those now far off days.

Contributor: Netta Murray is 81 years old and was born and bred in Kinsale. [Audio recording]

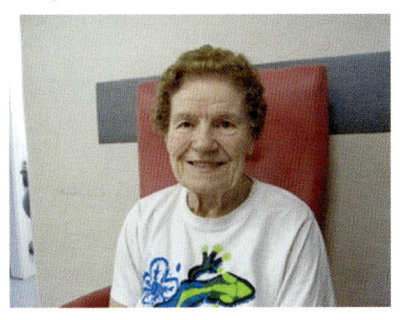

Netta Murray

Kinsale was very quiet in my time and things were very strict. In the summer evenings we were not allowed into town after 6pm. We could play in the street till 8.30 in the evening but we had to be in bed by

9, and we said the rosary every night. We loved walking all over the countryside, you'd see the old milk churns at the side of the road. They had the Latin Mass in those days, and the priest would read the gospel with his back to the congregation. The old mass.

My father was a butcher in Macroom. I loved growing up here, and I never left it except to go on a holiday. There were five in my family, and I had a twin sister, we were not identical. We were born in the Kinsale Hospital - the house over there was the mortuary. People had hens, and the hens would be out on the street. I love the chicks.

I worked in Tim Deasy's 56 years ago. This was before its time, offering gourmet foods, ground coffee, ground on the premises. The smell of fresh coffee was astounding, all over the town. I helped out in his shop and did the books. It was a deli, a very good deli. We had French people and German and Swiss people in Kinsale at that time, and he used to sell to them. We had snails which we sold in a plastic container, and the juice used to be at the bottom. The Swiss people would love figs, and Tim Deasy would order them for these Swiss people. They also wanted black bread or pumpernickel bread, and he would order that for them as well. I worked there for ten years until my mother became an invalid. I love figures.

That was over 50 years ago. Kinsale always had a lot of foreign people living here. At that time there was a lovely drapery shop and a grocery shop. There were very good drapery shops here, they were family-run. We had a lot of Americans as well, who bought the Aran sweaters. It was very cosmopolitan in those days as well.

Mylie Murphy and Cronin's were handed down within the family. I loved the atmosphere in Kinsale. People were very homely and friendly. You could leave the key in the door, and no one would bother with you. People were very neighbourly calling into each other and keeping an eye on each other, they'd have a chat and a cup of tea.

The regattas were very good in our day. You would meet people you hadn't seen for years. People came home for it, and it was a great weekend. There was a mart in Pearse Street, and they would arrive with their cows and everything. It was a great day. You would hardly have room to walk down the town on regatta day. We used to dress up for a prize. I came second twice. We used to dress up as the Royal Princesses.

We'd go walking mostly in our free time, as there wasn't a lot of activities. I never went dancing, my mother was strict and would not allow us. The harbour was lovely, we would go down to the pier every night before we went to bed. We would walk to Belgooly, and sometimes go by pony and tram. But even when I travelled I loved coming home. Scilly was a popular place for fishing. We used to play cards a lot, and the family rosary had to be said every night after tea. We would take a boat over to the Dock every Sunday and walk up to James Fort.

We used to have missions every year, and they used to frighten the life out of me. They were very morbid. They were in the Church, and there would be a sermon. It was all about our religion, and our faith They could be roaring at the pulpit. It was very frightening.

Contributor: Ann Daly (84), is a resident of Kinsale Hospital

Ann Daly

There was nothing there one time, no yachts in the sea. There was a lot more shops, you could buy absolutely anything in Kinsale then, but now there are only pubs and restaurants.

I worked at minding children, and I worked in Cronin's in Kinsale. It was very good. No cash registers in those days. The money was sent to the cashier via a little container attached to a pulley on the ceiling. I think the contraption is still there for the tourists to look at. I served the customers, not a lot of foreign people then. I started work at fifteen, because money was very scarce in those days, we were very poor, there was no money around. We used to go Kinsale on the bus from Belgooly. We had no car in those days, I only got a car when I got married in 1958. My husband was away at sea for years and then worked in Dublin, and he was retired when I married him. We had a nice time after that. I had one little boy. Unfortunately, I had twins first but they died. They were known as blue babies. There was nothing to be done at that stage and you just had to accept it.

I have lovely memories of working in Cronins, though we spent a lot of time on our knees keeping the place clean. I also worked in Murphy's Stores on Main Street and sold furniture. It was a lovely store and the family were salt of the earth and sold lovely furniture. They used to deliver the furniture to your house. You could get everything in Kinsale at one time and the shopkeepers were very good and they used to give credit to the poorer families. They were never expensive.

We went to dances in Minane Bridge and lots of concerts. There was very little money though in those days and women had to work very hard. We grew all our own vegetables, broccoli, new potatoes and all the vegetables. But things have got easier. But it was still nice then as we cycled everywhere, and got loads of fresh air, they were simpler times. There was plenty of work but the money was very poor.

There was seven in our family, but a few died of TB, it was rampant then.

I never travelled except to Dublin for my honeymoon. That was the only time I got out of Kinsale.

My family went to England and did very well. They went on a bicycle and came back with cars. My happiest time when I was growing up in Kinsale. The weather always seemed to be good but I suppose you only remember the good weather. We did a lot of walking and we did a lot cycling. We were very fit, so it was no bother to work hard, we ate simply, cabbage, spuds and porridge. Once you had porridge you were set up for the day. I left school at 14, and I went to work, that's what everybody did because you had to.

I lived through the war and a plane crashed near Kinsale. There were seven German soldiers in it, they took all their clothes off threw them into the burning plane, to be anonymous, and Seamus O'Neill took them in. He was able to speak all the languages, and he took them into Kinsale, he gave them everything. They were eventually sent to the Curragh in Kildare, treated well and returned to Germany after the war. They were so happy they landed in Ireland.

I am very happy to have lived through these times, and see things improved so much, and I would be very happy to go now as well. I am very happy in the hospital and it is home for me now, and I have lots of good memories.

Contributor: Matthew Geden was born in the English Midlands, moving to Kinsale in 1990. His most recent poetry collection is The Place Inside (Dedalus Press). He is the Director of Kinsale Writing School.

Winter in Kinsale

It's time now to take stock
of the dead; to sit before
the fire of all our gains
and losses, a red scrawl

flickering on the walls. In
the streets there is an absence
lurking behind every corner, each
time it catches me unawares

with its refusal to communicate,
the way it leaves words hanging.
It is said that strangers prosper here
so I act as strangely as I can,
laying siege to the dictionary
for explanations of where I am.
It's time now to take stock,
The old order is on the run.

Contributor: My name is Lynn Harding and my parents moved to Kinsale when they got married in 1983. [see George Harding] My siblings were both born there and although I was born in Cork city, I have spent half my life in Kinsale: every weekend, all summer, Christmas, Easter, Halloween... it is absolutely and completely my home, and my life's goal is to get back to live there full time. I work in Dublin now, but have never spent a summer without at least a few weeks in Kinsale; I even convinced my boss to let me rent an office and work down there for the summer a couple of years ago!

I wrote this poem not long after I first moved to Dublin. Plagued by homesickness, I was fed up of people in the big smoke telling me "we'd never guess you were from Cork by your accent!" I didn't take it as a compliment; it made me feel like I was thousands of miles from home, where nobody knew me at all.

[Lynn Harding's work has been published in Hennessy New Irish Writing in the Irish Times, and Poetry Ireland Review. She is a member of the Dublin Writers' Forum AH]

I come from a harbour town

Why can't we hear it in your voice?

The sea is a petrel song; you breathe out lead.

I speak faster

spray them with salt

flash a pebbled smile

promise mine is

a mother of pearl.

Why can't we see it in your face?

Your skin is powdered gypsum.
I pluck my brows to fishhooks
scrape my cheeks ruddy
with synthetic sand
nightly wash the foamy swell
surging to the plughole.

Why don't you wear it on your back?
Kinsale sports a cape.

I furl myself
in linen, greys and greens,
waive my curls to the wind
to whip into a whirlpool.

Why don't you swim away?
You're only treading water.

I traipse the prom
trawl sandy coves for witnesses
skim grey stones
leap forty feet into the surf.

Outdoor Kinsale

Contributor: Adrian Wistreich (See above – Chasing the Dream)

Morning in Kinsale

It's just after seven on a fine bright June morning. We drive down the lane to the little stone bridge opposite White Castle, and onto the road that runs alongside an inlet of the Bandon River – the road which avoids driving through town – and over the causeway. At this time of the morning, there's a stream of cars headed for Eli Lilly. They must all start work at 7.30, which means there'll be a steady stream in the opposite direction between 3.30 and 5.00pm, But we're the only car headed for the Dock this morning, it seems. We cross the causeway, water lapping the stone walls and seemingly above the level of the road, and continue along past the mussel beds which have been developed again after years of inactivity on the river bend. Apparently, the Bandon river supplied oysters for all of Cork in the 19th century. We go straight past The Marsh, now covered by ever-growing housing estates, and around the foot of Compass Hill, to the layby beside the new bridge, which of an evening is thronged with holiday-makers and locals looking for fresh 'Catch of the Day', or an authentic clay oven-baked pizza. But at sunrise, the area is empty, save for one or two stalwarts making use of the new outdoor gymnasium on the river bank.

We cross the bridge and turn left to the Dock. It's a journey I've made most days for the last eighteen years, with one or other of the dogs we host for Irish Guide Dogs for the Blind. Since Aby arrived from Switzerland, a Labrador with a special responsibility to produce puppies for guide dog training, it's become easier, since she was trained more thoroughly than any of her predecessors. As we approach the end of the road, she stirs in the back of the car, knowing we're getting close. She probably hears gulls or feels familiar bumps in the road. In the winter it's a two-way street, but from June it's meant to be one-way down to the beach with the return journey requiring everyone to drive over the top of the hill towards the graveyard and De Courcy Castle. It's superficially irritating to have to travel further in the summer, but what other reason would there be to view Kinsale from the top? Of course, plenty of early risers ignore the signs, and drive back along the waterside, but you learn to keep an eye out for cars coming the wrong way. Down near the pub there are a couple of camper vans whose sleeping occupants are oblivious to the wonders of the early morning sun over the Dock Marina, and the gentle clacking of wire on masts.

We park at the corner where there's a 'no overnight parking' sign by the slipway – you'd be wary leaving a car when there's spring tides – and head up by the ruined cottage. There's been rumours of renovations, but still the fuchsia grows through its windows.

Aby drags and dawdles over the familiar smells left by previous visitors she knows. The steep path takes us around the back of James Fort and up to the top field, where the hay has just been cut. We both know the paths and ruts intimately, and our pace matches the glorious day – it's up-beat and rhythmic. The sun is piercing and the light is sharp. There isn't a cloud to be seen above us. From the gap in the hedge, we can see Heineken Heights and that mansion which Nama, or was it the CAB, re-possessed some years back from that property developer who disappeared off to South Africa, and that wonderful terrace of slated houses at the bottom of the Scilly walk, where the Spinnaker used to be, and where the Harbour Bar still snuggles between all the new glass and concrete fortresses.

The colours are shrieking at us across the water. All the lines are crisp and everything is delineated by edges, and those intense dark shadows. The water is what watercolourists like to call azure blue, and the chrome-topped gunwales in the marina sparkle and flash. The lush hanging baskets around town punctuate the harbour walls with vibrant reds and deep purples, a quarter of a mile away. There's something down there in the water, bobbing between the buoys. Maybe a seal, or perhaps a cormorant looking for breakfast. There's barely a breath of wind across the top of the James Fort hill, which opens onto the panorama on the far side of the fort and the bay below. From here, I can see the mouth of the harbour, the still water, just rippling from the strong currents out past Charles Fort to the Boatyard. In front of me, the multi-coloured enclave of Summercove is painted and still. It's too early for any visible activity in sleepy Summercove.

The dog isn't interested in the magnificence of this view. She's seen a friend across both fields, coming up from the Dock Beach, and is only happy to crouch and wait, rather than bowling down to meet him. I'd know the gait of his owner from here. I know what he'll say when we meet, and what I'll reply. Same greetings every morning, same smile, just a moment of familiarity. There'll be more encounters before we get back to the car. There'll be that guy who likes to swim naked, though he's been getting here earlier and earlier to avoid embarrassment as he emerges from the foam. There'll be those inevitable campers with their empties from last night, and maybe a few charred sausages forgotten in the grass. There'll be sand between the toes and spatters of sea-water where Aby has shaken herself onto my leg after the swim. There'll be the drive home and the morning news. The anticipation of coffee and getting the dog's breakfast. There'll be the day ahead. But first, up here, at the top by the fort, looking out across the morning, there'll be that moment. When I know. When it all comes together in one overwhelming feeling. I belong here.

Contributor: <u>Cara</u> McDonagh is ten years old and was born and raised in Kinsale. She attends Gaelscoil Chionn tSaile.

Snowed In!

I know lots of kids who will read this book and think 'Is there gonna be any kids writing in this book?'. I know because I'm a kid, and I'm going to write about the snow that happened in March. Some people when they talk about the snow, they go on about electricity bills and heating and whatnot. But that's boring. I mean, what about the sun?

We've never had proper snow. Not since I was two. When I think of snow I think of the dribbles we usually get. But imagine the excitement when we heard we were getting proper snow in Kinsale! Me and my friends had conversations like this:

'Did you hear about the snow?'

'Yeah! Me and my brothers are going sledding.'

'You're crazy! I hate sledding!'

'What? Oh my God, she doesn't like sledding!'

'Guys shut up and get on with the game!'

When it happened, we were in our apartment, a beautiful place by the harbour (where nobody seemed to live) and we were, well, ... unprepared. A week beforehand, my mum went to the Bandon Co-op and couldn't find any sleds. When she asked the lady who worked there, she said:

'Oh, sorry, we're all sold out!'

When it came, I was asleep. Lying there, asleep (I was probably dreaming), when I heard them talking. My brothers I mean. I couldn't quite make out what they were saying. I figured out about a minute later when they burst into my room shouting:

'Cara, There's Snow!'

'Snow?' I said groggily.

I peeked out the window. Wow, there was snow everywhere! On the pavement, the plants, the windows! I ran out of my room, 'Can I go outside?' I asked my parents.

'Sure,' they said, 'Just put on your hat, your coat, your gloves and your boots!'

'Yes!' I said.

The snow was lovely. Squishy, but it still made a lovely crunch sound. I loved the way it felt when I tried to make a snow angel (twice, unsuccessfully). Then we went sledding at James Fort Walk. Of course we didn't have any sleds, so we used bin bags, At the start we couldn't move so we just looked silly. But eventually, we started to move.

Afterwards we went to The Dock, which is a nice pub next to the fort and the beach. We had drinks and crisps before going home. Later, the next day, we wandered into Kinsale. It was lovely in the snow. The pharmacy was especially pretty as it had window displays as well. And the Blue Haven had its big nutcrackers outside, so it looked made for snow.

We also played with friends that day and had snowball fights near the local Supervalu. Me and my friend agreed: Kinsale in the snow is awesome!

Contributor: Daniel Galvin is 23, and has had his writing published in <u>The Moth</u>, <u>The Rose</u>, <u>Pulsar</u>, <u>Hidden Channel</u>, <u>Cold Coffee Stand</u> and <u>The Scum Gentry</u>. He came first place in the Spoken Word Platform at Cuirt International Literary Festival 2017, and won the May 2017 Sunday Slam in Dublin. Daniel performed poetry sets at Electric Picnic, 2017 and will read at the 2018 Words by Water festival in Kinsale. He is currently working towards his first poetry collection.

He explains his connection to Kinsale: I grew up Ballinspittle area but attended secondary school in Kinsale and work in the town. My great great Grandfather on my mother's side, Hugh Wright, was disowned by his Protestant family in Monaghan when he converted to Catholicism, and absconded to Kinsale to marry local girl Mary Kelly around 1900. I don't know how far back the Kelly line goes in the town.

Snow Day

Scarf for my balaclava,

I swung my school shoes up and over,

clearing the gate tops,

snow flying around.

Real snow now

and those who remained in class

could only watch it fall

and us go

darting down old people streets

screaming scumbag, maggot, mistletoe and wine

though it was late January, and the lights had been taken down.
We sang it in the car parks
and in the playground from our stage atop the climbing frame,
then we pissed on all the slides.

Later, we went to the steepest hill around
with our surf boards and hubcaps
and crunched to the top, again and again
until the message came
that a beer delivery lorry had been left open and unattended
down the Glen for all of five minutes
and I and two others were nominated
and we did not return empty handed,
slipping and sliding away with it all
under yellow lamplight blooming.

Heatwave

The ground turns hard against my father's boot.

His breathless, bleached-sick paddocks glare.

Forecasts stretch in sunny absolutes

and murmurs walk the swollen air.

Past the drone of prayers for rain

that burn up in the heat of day,

I cross the bridge of bobbing sterns

from choking fields to the boats of Kinsale

and the Harbour bar where talk runs thick

beside a sculptured pool of stone—

carved in stone, a bird and chick

sipping nothing from the parched bowl.

Contributor: Marcia Wrixon lives in Sandycove, and is known for her occasional verse. A collection of her work, <u>Love is for the Birds</u> was published in 2011.

Photo credit: Sheena Jolley's 'Seagull'

Sandycove Covenant

If there's a God, it's surely here
He hides his face, where mists ascend
In curtained light without an end
And contours blur which once were clear.
The seabourn cloud and rainbow's arc
Modify both light and dark.

In Genesis the waters part, and Earth
Is separate, as night from day.
But here, where men and goats might play
Satyrical in moments filled with mirth,
The promised land by turns is wet and dried
Then distanced once again by rising tide.

The changeling sea which has no fixed abode
Illusively extends its silken reach
And quietly might rearrange the beach
Or with a flourish, airily explode,
The heartlong surge of waves upon the shore,
Turning time and tide to metaphor.

Circling slowly the cove around
A gull appears in the prismatic sky
Fragmenting the air with a sudden cry
Comic and cosmic in its mocking sound.
After the echo, a dove-grey hush
And only the hint of a feather's brush.

Contributor: Grace O'Doherty is a 23 year old writer from Wicklow. She recently completed the MA Writing at NUI Galway. Her work has been published or is forthcoming in Banshee, Stony Thursday Poetry Anthology, Mouldy Bike Periodical and headstuff.org. She was chosen to participate in the Poetry Mentorship Programme at Cúirt International Festival of Literature 2018 and read at their Spotlight on New Voices event.

She writes: while I've only been living in Kinsale for a few months, my father's mother's family come from Ballinspittle. I would have visited Kinsale and the surrounding countryside often as a child, calling on relatives, coming into town for the funfair and fish and chips in Dino's. I hope you'll enjoy reading the poem, which was inspired by wanderings through the beautiful scenery around Sandy Cove area.

Out Towards Sandycove

I must have been a child when I visited this place

or somewhere like it.

Bungalows coloured

damp peach of dreams, gull's beak yellow,

blue of bathrooms and greens not often seen

in the natural world.

My heart runs out to meet

the just-out-of-dateness of decor:

long-lost beige arm of couch,

drooping head

of a lampshade at the window.

ii

Face, blurred pale thumbprint,

of the shawled woman in an unmarked photo.

The way I heard somebody talking

about somebody else

fondly and sadly

in the voice of a memory getting smaller and smaller.

iii

I don't know the road well enough

to say if it will bring me

here or there:

flared cliff edge,

line of houses rearing up from the pier.

iv

The sea is not always there.

It disappears around corners.

I stick to the track.

When it's dark in this neck of the woods

you see real stars.

Contributor: Sheila Forde (See Kinsale Memories)

Billy Divers' Conference

Sunrise at Sandycove Island a dark gathering

Shading the reflections of the sea

Over the cove all the way to the creek.

A cormorant dives somersaults swoops low

Others follow nosediving the water in hundreds

Like blackbirds falling from the sky

Filling the sea between the island and the mainland

Childhood memories come flooding back

Of watching those great black birds swooping

Disappearing for several minutes

Re-surfacing with their catch of the day.

Cormorant a difficult word to say
And hence the name Billy Divers.

Occasional dives and somersaults
Disappearing resurfacing with fish wedged between beaks
Quickly swallowed.
Chatter intensifying creating clicking echoing sound
Feathers glistening from the sun's rays
Reflecting oil slick image echoing sounds to the island
And my viewing wall.

Sounds of multiple chats before the meeting begins
Swapping places flapping wings, kissing beaks.
Each enthusiastic to find the perfect handsome mate.
Gazing out to the sea of black a voice beside me whispers
Is this the Billy Divers' Conference?

Contributor: Kevin Cahill: I have lived most of life in Kinsale (Catholic Walk and River Meadows) or surrounding areas. I currently live between Ballinspittle and Garretstown. My family connections with the town stretch back through several generations. Kinsale holds many memories for my family and I, of the past and in the present.

The first poem, <u>Sabbatical on Sandycove Island</u>, is somewhat imagined but it represents an evening my wife and I spent watching the sun retreat out in Sandycove.

The second poem, <u>Commogue</u>, was written when I was living in River Meadows. While we were living there the Commogue marsh was transformed by the building of estate after estate. The view from our front room there in River Meadows was down towards the marsh through the branches of a resilient birch tree.

Sabbatical on Sandycove Island

Moonlit moorings marked our course.

Soft lapping ripples rocked us,

As we rowed stroke for stroke

Through the black glaze of time's

Tense harbour doors.

The tide-shaped coast afforded comfort

To our travels.

Our island berth grew larger,

Then everything faded.

Alone. Together in the darkness.

Fate foraged our path.

Hand-to-hand we waded ashore.
No words left our lips that night,
None were needed.

A goat stood silhouetted on the skyline.
A fellow exile. Forced, yet grown
Homely amid the gorse. What twist
Of fate pulled us together?
And now to here?

Our other island. Home from home.
We had stepped back into the nothingness.
No sunlight but silver
Moon monuments lighting the way to Cúirtaporteen.
No motor hums,
But aural ebb and flow. Rhythmic. Real.

The warmth of our embrace, embraced
Everything. Still silent, lips touched lips
And the sun rose above the hill to peak upon us.
The goat grumbled and galloped,
Away to morning feed.

The same signposts steered us home that morning.
Back to silence. More crossed between us in the silence
Of that night than in the five years of talking across the
Flecked black and white kitchen counter-top.

Home again, we smiled a knowing smile,
Slipped into the morning suits and sailed
Along the R600 to the humdrum downtown
Of the everyday. Outside, the clouds made the shape
Of a goat flouncing on the morning sky.

Commogue

Skeletal remains of the once,

And will be again, blooming birch,

Breaks the chimney pot turreted skyline.

"Gross lack of foresight planting her here",

Where predators lurch.

Spoils the view of "custom-built

Twenty-first century accommodation",

That's what it says on the sign.

Now syncopated strums of heavy

Machinery shudder through the undergrowth.

Even the tea in my teacup ripples

As the post-historic Krakens crane

To feed from the River Bandon moat.

Preternatural pincers preying deep into

Our Land of Heart's Desire.

Centuries have sailed by since this

Once oaken paradise

Was pounced and pillaged in the name

Of King, Country and commerce,

Tongue-slicing seafarers gorged on

The age like wood-lice.

And now, once more, and army

Workman clothed, construct an empire

Of slate and brick and shoddy plaster.

Tyranny repeats itself, defeats itself,

Dies and waits for rebirth.

"Down tools and go home", are the

Orders from the Union.

I'll wait by the lounge room window,

Until the hearth goes out, then set again

For the inevitable dawn intrusion.

Commogue will wake,

Not with gull cry and heron call

But cranes and diggers,

Hazing up the morning sun.

Contributor: Alannah Hopkin - see Editor's Introduction

This piece was broadcast in Lyric FM's Quiet Quarter in 2003, and included in The Quiet Quarter Anthology of New Irish Writing *(New Island, 2004) edited by Eoin Brady.*

Swimming Round the Island

We are lucky in Kinsale, because we have an ideal swimming place, Sandy Cove. There is a channel about 300 metres across, between the mainland and a small island, uninhabited apart from a flock of wild goats. We swim across to the island and back, and every so often there is an organised swim with rescue boats and proper safety precautions, around the island.

The swimming season starts in June. The first swim of the year is cold enough to hurt, but the trick is not to give up, to swim through the pain barrier. One of the great pleasures of sea swimming is that all you need is a comfortable swimsuit, a rubber hat and a pair of goggles. Only wimps swim in wet suits in the summer.

I first swam around the island, a distance of a mile and a bit, on a calm August evening two years ago. I was apprehensive, because I do not swim the crawl, I swim breaststroke, slowly. I am what serious head-down swimmers call 'a sightseer' – I like to look at the scenery and the wild life as I swim. It takes me about forty-five minutes to swim a mile, compared to about twenty minutes for a fast swimmer. But I love it.

You push off from the quay along with the rest of the slow group, maybe ten other swimmers, and head out around the western end of the island to the open sea.

There is a wonderful moment when you pass the tip of the island, when all you can see up ahead is sea, sea as far as the horizon. You forget about the other swimmers, the spectators, the rescue boats, your husband on the point with binoculars, your sister on the quay worrying, everything goes. There is just you, and the sea. It is at once the loneliest and the most exciting feeling – there is just you, a small insignificant mammal, two arms and two legs working away, and this vast, black sea. What am I doing here? The scale is awesome.

Going down the outside of the island is quite different from swimming in its shelter. The surge is much stronger, but not unpleasant. On a big, organised swim, we disturb the nesting gulls, who fly overhead in great shrieking flocks.

The first time around, you learn a cruel fact: the east end of the island is not a point, like its west end, but it is another side. The island is a triangle, not an oval, as it appears from land. But the views are good, and you know there is sheltered water, waiting around the corner.

Back in the inner harbour there are still about fifteen minutes to go. By now I have caught my third wind, a great moment, when you know for sure that you can keep on until you're back at the quay, and hardly a feather out of you. Maybe it's adrenaline, or the famous endorphin high – whatever it is, it's nice.

And then, when you come to the slip, and you are among the last home, still swimming your leisurely breaststroke, which has become automatic, like a reflex action by this stage, the kindly spectators give a big cheer as you get out of the water and stand on dry land again and you feel, just for a nanosecond, like a hero. Your muscles are toned and stretched, you heart beat is low and steady, you feel good, very good. Within seconds you are shivering uncontrollably, teeth chattering loudly, but it was great, and you'd do it again anytime. Honestly, it was great, I enjoyed it, you keep saying, and the non-swimmers shake their heads in disbelief.

Contributor: Writer and journalist Gemma Tipton has lived in Kinsale for ten years, after falling in love with it on a weekend visit and never managing to fully leave. She works with the Irish Times, while also writing for numerous Irish and international magazines. She has published books, appears on radio and television, and for two years was Guest Artistic Director of the Kinsale Arts Festival.

Dead Cat Corner

Bosco was an urban horse. We met when he was four; unafraid of double decker busses, JCBs and fire engines, he had been destined for the dog food factory. With reasonable, but unspectacular breeding, he was meant to be a racehorse, but a small personality quirk had kept him from that goal. Bosco has a nervous fear of being the Last Horse In The World, and so when he gets out in front, he slows down and waits for his mates to catch up. If he's too far ahead, he'll stop dead. Charming in a riding horse, it's quite fatal on the track.

Life isn't necessarily kind to an unsuccessful thoroughbred. In the beginning he wouldn't let anyone touch his head, ducking away, expecting a clout. Apples would eventually get the better of him. He also didn't understand the point of trotting, all his training had been about standing pent-up still, and then racing, flat out. Going round a sand arena in circles taught patience to both of us.

We first came to Kinsale when he was eight. He had just been competing in the Polocrosse National Finals. Not with me, I had lent him to a friend and, when she dropped him down, he pranced out of the horsebox in his matching rug and travel boots, looking like an equine supermodel. I felt very proud, as if owning something of such beauty could lend me a share in beauty's magic.

The next morning we went riding. In Dublin you can ride in a covered school or arena, and for a few short summer months, have a gallop up the long side of a short field. Longer hacks mean horsebox journeys, and avoiding the proliferating signs: on beaches, on forestry tracks, on pathways; telling you you're not welcome. Sometimes, out of desperation, we would trot to the nearby shopping park, and down Costa Coffees while the horses munched exhaust-flavoured grass on the verge.

In Kinsale, we rode down the winding lane, and on to Charles Fort, which would, once upon a time, have housed a regiment of horses. Then up the hill and out, beyond the Boat Yard to the shooting range. In a stubble field that seemed to be going on forever, and yet simultaneously falling off the edge of the world, we stopped to watch the waves lapping at The Sovereigns. Kestrels flew up from below the cliffs, the sea stretched out, and the sky felt alive.

Bosco had more on his mind than the view. "Shall we fly up the hill?" my new friend asked. Her pony clearly knew the drill. Horses don't do views in the way that humans do. And so we did. Maybe there's just one thing that everyone, human, bird or animal, was born to do perfectly. If there is, we're lucky if we find it. When a thoroughbred runs, you know what theirs is. Bosco's tensed up prancing switches to speed. It's called flat out, because he does flatten out, body going lower to the ground as he races. Then, he pauses, measuring his speed, because he's already inseparable from Pepper, his pony mate, who he had just met yesterday, and with whom he will soon become irritatingly obsessed.

How do you store something like that up? Make a pocket in your memory for it? I felt indescribably, unbelievably lucky to be there. The track up, running parallel to the long field, crests, and then you turn left for home. Horse-height is perfect for hedgerow hacks. I'm told it's the same distance up as the cab in an articulated lorry, but it's only on a horse that you have a slower, peaceful passage, seeing across the fields, into gardens, saying hello to small dogs, and sitting deep in the saddle as you pass fluttering underpants on windy washing lines.

Unafraid of heavy lorries he may have been, but Bosco took an instant dislike to cows. He was also highly sceptical of chickens, and suspicious of the sea. Soon, in spite of this, a favourite ride became to wander along to Lower Cove for a slither down the pebbly beach, to splash about in the sea. At first, it was only Pepper's paddling that persuaded Bosco in, but he got used to it, and now, standing in blue-green waters, as ripples run by your horse's hocks and sailboats drift past, is sublime.

In time you get to know the route. There's Dead Cat corner, where we found not one but two dead felines on subsequent weeks. Lost Stirrup Field, where a brilliant gallop was made suddenly lopsided. When we were eventually able to rein in, we retraced, like forensic searchers, until we found the missing tack, glinting in the stubble.

One day we met Boris. A coloured, opinionated pony, Boris had a temporary residence on the end of a long tether line in the fallow ground beside Charles Fort. It seemed a good spot for him. There was plenty of grass, though, his owner told us, it could become hazardous when well-intentioned people tried to feed him crisps and sandwiches. Boris and Bosco felt an immediate and profound need to impress one another: Boris running crazed bucking laps at the end of his tether,

Bosco cavorting sideways, oblivious to traffic. "What if his rope snaps?" my friend asked drily. It never did. In time they settled down, and we missed Boris when he eventually moved on. Before he went, he made a visit to The Bulman, somewhere Bosco has never been, though it's one of my favourite pubs.

Bosco is seventeen now. He's still not crazy about cows, but quite at home with hens. Birds of prey don't bother him, and he's made his peace with the sea. More fields than there used to be are now closed off to riders, even though we are always careful only to enter when the crops are cut. Still, riding out from home, adventuring on four hooves, going places without the intervention of a horsebox, has to be one of the most fundamental pleasures of having a horse. Something humans have done for millennia, it would be a great shame if it ever ceased completely. Bosco and I were meant to come to Kinsale for a month, but we never left. I don't know if horses dream, but I don't think either of us could ever have dreamed of this: winding lanes, acres upon acres of golden stubble, swooping birds, the smooth moving sea, and fields that run off the edge of the world.

Contributor: George Harding (see Kinsale Memories)

Scatter Me

Do not send me down
but scatter me
over the seal's cave,
and if his old grey head
should emerge to say hello
just say goodbye instead.

Do not lie me down
but scatter me
around the Chieftain's grave
and if you see that old grey fox
slinking down the path
give him one last wave.

Do not put me down
but scatter me
on Ballymacus sod
and if you hear the lilting lark
above the heathered glen
tell him I'll applaud.

Index

Index of Contributors

Broderick, Christina, 60

Browne, Fergal, 175, 193

Cahill, Kevin, 246

Cargin, Charlotte, 43

Clayton, Alan, 17

Connon, Dearbhail, 62

Creed, Elizabeth, 53

Cronin, Brian, 37

Eaton, Paul, 59

Forde, Sheila, 204, 244

Frey, Peter, 13

Geden, Matthew, 228

Galvin, Christina, 201

Galvin, Daniel, 238

Hall, Malcolm, 51

Hall, William, 218

Harding, George, 257

Harding, Lynn 229

Index of Contributors Cont.

Harvey, Klaus, 183

Herlihy, Donal, 217

Holley, Veronica, 8

Hopkin, Alannah, 63, 251

Hunt, Rod, 7

Ibbotson, Linda, 11

Lalor, Brian, 180

Lordan, Jerome, 35

Mahon, Derek, 25

McDonagh, Cara, 236

McGlinchey, Afric, 22

McGouran, Bernard, 186

Moloney, Barry, 46

Moody, Paul, 24

Murray, Netta, 223

O'Doherty, Grace, 242

Renwick, Robin, 208

Ryan, Dermot, 192

Index of Contributors Cont.

Shanahan, Martin, 33

Thuillier, John, 173

Tipton, Gemma, 253

Waldron, Siobhan, 7

Wistreich, Adrian, 41, 233

Wrixon, Marcia, 241

Young, Augustus, 214

Young, John, 19